This Is My Story, This Is My Song, THIS IS MY MIRACLE

JAMES W. STORY

Printed in the United States of America.

All Scripture quotations, unless otherwise indicated, are taken from the Holy Bible, New International Version ®, NIV®. Copyright©1973, 1978, 1984, 2011 by Biblica, Inc.™ Used by permission of Zondervan. All rights reserved worldwide. www.zondervan.com. The "NIV" and "New International Version" are trademarks registered in the United States Patent and Trademark Office by Biblica, Inc.™

All prayers, unless written by the author, are printed with the permission of Lisa Weathers Hall, who wrote prayers for each step of the author's battle with COVID-19.

Grateful acknowledgment is made to members of the author's family who lovingly shared their memories through conversations and family records.

Photographs courtesy of the Story family

Cover designed by Bruce Gore | Gore Studio

Edited by Judy H. Jones, with contributions by Rev. Norman Hall and Barbara Snell

Print ISBN: 978-1-66780-885-7
eBook ISBN: 978-1-66780-886-4

This book is dedicated to my mother, Naomi

Table of Contents

Introduction 1

PART I 7

Chapter 1: "For the Beauty of the Earth" 9

Chapter 2: Understanding the African Culture of My Ancestry 11

Chapter 3: The Andersons: Their Story, Their Song................14

Chapter 4: The Storys: Their Story, Their Song................17

Chapter 5: "Lead Me, Guide Me" 20

Chapter 6: The Hamiltons: Their Story, Their Song................22

Chapter 7: "On a Hill Far Away" 26

Chapter 8: "Will the Circle Be Unbroken?" 30

Chapter 9: "What a Friend We Have in Jesus" 35

Chapter 10: Summertime................38

Chapter 11: Church Music................43

PART II 45

Chapter 12: My Musical Mentors: Their Stories, Their Songs................47

Chapter 13: Integration - Unity in Action 56

Chapter 14: "Pass Me Not O Gentle Savior"................59

Chapter 15: "This Little Light of Mine"................61

Chapter 16: "Sometimes I Feel Like a Motherless Child" 66

Chapter 17: "How Firm a Foundation" 70

Chapter 18: "On Eagle's Wings" 75

Chapter 19: Breaking Down Barriers 80

PART III 85

    Chapter 20: Angels...87

    Chapter 21: Perseverance.......................................90

    Chapter 22: "Love Now"..93

    Chapter 23: "Circle of Life" 98

    Chapter 24: "Sweet Hour of Prayer" 103

    Chapter 25: Face to Face 106

    Chapter 26: The Valley.. 109

    Chapter 27: My Battle with COVID-19 Timeline.............................. 112

    Chapter 28: Step by Step - Road to Recovery 117

    Chapter 29: Moments of Encouragement... 119

    Chapter 30: The Healing Power of Music 122

    Chapter 31: The Recovery Process — Facebook Entries..................... 126

    Chapter 32: Short Journal Entries.. 130

    Chapter 33: For Good.. 133

    Chapter 34: Prayer, Healing, and Hope... 136

    Chapter 35: A COVID-19 Survivor's Prayer 139

    Chapter 36: From Hoax to Hope.. 141

    Chapter 37: The Light and the Leaf 143

    Chapter 38: "There's a Miracle in You".. 145

    Chapter 39: Going Home.. 147

References 151

Introduction

THIS IS MY **STORY** AS A BLACK man; this is my **song** as a musician; this is my **miracle** as a COVID-19 survivor.

Perhaps fittingly, I was born on a Sunday, December 18, 1955, in Greeneville, Tennessee. I would like to think I was ushered into the world with the sounds of angelic melodies, sanctified handclaps, tambourines, and organs, but I doubt it was that pleasant. Nevertheless, the calm and foggy December air settled amongst the mountains to announce Season's Greetings. The excitement and anticipation of Christmas embraced the town.

Life is slow in Greeneville. So much so, that time can often feel like an illusion. Nestled in the foothills of the Appalachian Mountains, the Nolichucky River winding nearby, my hometown is concealed by great hills and grand trees in all their glory. Only the train tracks serve as a reminder that there, indeed, is a world beyond our hills. If you were not looking for Greeneville, you might never find it.

I have taken up the quest of being the hand holding the pen and writing my story—that of a young boy from these mountains of East Tennessee dreaming of playing music. As I share my own story, I am eager to share stories of my ancestors and musical mentors who have had a hand in guiding my path to becoming a musician and an educator.

In Part I of this book, I pay homage to my family and particularly my ancestors who endured the degradation of being taken from their homeland, the danger of crossing an ocean on slave ships, and the humiliation of the auction block, and yet maintained their dignity. They overcame extreme hardships and created a life worth living in a foreign land by using their innate music and dance talents to work through hardship, overcome obstacles, celebrate victories, and create joy. They utilized their agricultural skills to support their families and communities and express thankfulness for the Earth and its bounty. They echoed dignity and community through their spirituality and their ability—perhaps against all odds—to sustain faith in God and gratitude for their existence.

I have always relished the stories passed down through generations of my family. As my elders shared their stories of hardships, I envisioned their lives filled with strife and pain but also with strength and even triumph. These elders told stories of learning to read and write in one-room schoolhouses (if they were allowed to learn to read), ancestors born out of wedlock as children of slave masters, some being sold away and married off from their family by their slave masters, and others born and raised on Native American reservations. I was and still am intrigued with their lives, their stories, and our culture. Their low socioeconomic status and the commonly perpetuated myth of inferiority based on their Blackness, the depth of their skin color, mixed blood, and slave-labor roots shaded their life experience in East Tennessee. I inherited this experience along with those vibrant stories and rich culture.

My longing to understand the stories of my relatives, listen to them, feel them, be entrusted with them, and share them has consumed me since my youth when storytelling seemed to be in such abundance. Any holiday, family reunion, funeral, Sunday supper, or church gathering included an exchange of stories and lively display of storytelling. Passed down through oral traditions, I bore witness to some stories, while others were shrouded in mystery, secrecy, strife, taboo, and disappointment.

My elders were the keepers of our past long before the history books; therefore, my elders were my best teachers. Through the stories they shared, I can better understand my reality as a boy growing up in the Jim Crow South. Struggling to understand the strong hold that hate and prejudice had on us, the elders always seemed to have an anecdote that provided perspective.

Some of their stories are at risk of slipping into obscurity simply because they are not being passed along. My mission to piece these narratives together has consumed my soul as the stories have twisted, turned, unraveled, and unfolded in preparation for this memoir. This is my gift to future generations of my family. Whatever we accomplish, we must acknowledge that we stand on the shoulders of our ancestors.

In my hometown of Greeneville, Tennessee, Blacks were treated differently than the Whites. Blacks comprised the lowest of the southern caste system, and the inequality was evident because Blacks were excluded from certain places and activities. Specific rules applied to Blacks and not to other people. Our forefathers communicated these narratives through oral traditions—stories steeped in mystery, family struggles, and disappointments, some still playing out in my lifetime. By chronicling their narratives, this memoir reveals how my forebearers' lives, especially as musicians and educators, have impacted my life.

Our family roots run deep on both my maternal and paternal sides. According to DNA testing (https://www.23andme.com), I am part of a priesthood lineage that dates to Pharaoh Ramesses III, a product of sub-Saharan Africa dating to more than a millennium before European colonization of America and the Atlantic slave trade. My African ancestors resided in the area extending from Senegal to Nigeria to Egypt, a richly populated area of 307 million people and home to hundreds of distinct ethnic groups. The groups were united under a series of powerful empires, resulting in broad similarities in music, clothing, art, and cuisine. My research reveals that my ancestors were Nigerian, Ghanaian, Liberian and Sierra Leonean, Senegambian, Guinean, Congolese, and Southern East African. To my surprise, I also have

British and Irish ancestors who evolved from the Celtic, Saxon, and Viking people, and I have links to Native American Indians and people of East Asian descent. These diverse cultures are part of my DNA, my heritage, my people, and, most of all, my music.

As I think about my history, I realize that the New World African brought with him not just his physical presence but also the content of his mind–his memory. He had a thought process crafted by his homeland. He didn't just have to learn a new language in a foreign land, but he also had to adapt to the new land's value system which was different than what his previous life had taught him. While trying to survive in this unfamiliar environment, the African would have found reassurance in clinging desperately to his native African value system–an ancient system of beliefs, ideas, and behaviors. These attributes had been tested and honed by countless preceding generations. They could not easily be discarded.

Could the saga of the Black mountaineers who made East Tennessee their home answer some of my many questions about my existence—about who I am? Whether they sought out these mountains or were born here, they settled in these hills and left their mark in these hills. From these hills they passed on their legacy to new generations. The stories of these Black mountaineers are my story.

I began genealogical research to understand my ancestors and the influence of music in my culture. As I studied my family history, I discovered that many of my ancestors were musicians. Could the influence and miraculous power of this ancient art form somehow transcend through the ages and create *my* passion for music? I could see how the rich blessings of music—the words and melodies of songs I heard as a youngster—had shaped my life. Songs were part of the oral traditions passed down by my elders. I felt the connection.

Music was vital to my community, church, home, and school while I was growing up in a small town in East Tennessee. How fortunate was I! My father, aunts, and uncles all participated in church music. Part II of this book goes on to describe how my elementary teachers laid a solid foundation for teaching music in my formative years. With the joy of learning music and my high regard for this new language, I found my destiny. By the end of my elementary school years, I had found my profession. I knew I would become a music educator.

I continued to hone my musical talents through high school and college. I followed my passion, and I was blessed with many opportunities to display and improve my skills.

Since college, I have always held a part-time church job. This work has not been done out of financial necessity, but out of a desire to serve the Lord. The church music ministry is a significant part of my spiritual life. Creating and blending musical sounds with voices and instruments—forming interchanges of spiritual offerings—has brought more blessings to me than I could ever have imagined. I have had so many "out-of-body" and "mountaintop" experiences while conducting instrumental and vocal ensembles throughout my life. At times, the music would well up inside me and flow down my arms to my fingertips onto the ivory piano keys or to the tip of my conducting baton.

My tribute to my ancestors and musical influences originally did not include Part III of this narrative. However, the lessons of my elders and overwhelming power of music were gamechangers in my battle against COVID-19. God gave me another chapter in my life to share with others.

When I retired in 2018, ending my forty-two-year teaching career, my objective was to slow down and recreate my music career. I wanted to establish my own musical goals and resume projects that had been on hold because of time constraints. I had expected to have more control of my life and become more protective of my time; however, I found myself on a treadmill of trying to be everything to everybody in my professional life and immediate family life as well. My pre-pandemic life had gotten so busy that I was as active as I had been working my full-time job at Volunteer State Community College *and* my part-time/full-time position as the music director at the First United Methodist Church in Gallatin, Tennessee. Then the pandemic hit, and suddenly everything stopped.

I share my faith, trials, and victory of surviving COVID-19 in the closing chapters of this book. Developed in a devotional format, these chapters include stories of hope mixed with my favorite songs and the music that helped me along my healing journey. I credit my amazing healthcare workers for my healing, but scriptures, prayers, songs, and music were instrumental in my recovery. I pray that my experience gives hope to those who have suffered or may suffer from the coronavirus—a virus that has taken the lives of more than 4.7 million people around the world as this book goes to press.

As I began the slow rehabilitation process, I began to post on Facebook to keep friends and family updated on my recovery progress and to dispel rumors surrounding my extended hospital stay. Also, I was seeking prayer for my healing. To my surprise, people around the world set up prayer vigils for my recovery. People became closer through this simple act of worship. My "near-death" experience became a powerful testimony to the goodness of God and His mercy. During my journey, I knew God was and is still in control.

There is Hope in Christ Jesus.

—James W. Story

THIS IS MY STORY

PART I

CHAPTER 1:

"For the Beauty of the Earth"

THERE ARE SO MANY BEAUTIFUL mountains globally, but none more majestic than the Appalachian Mountains of Eastern Tennessee. They are rich in folklore and captivating stories of times past. The mountain rivers flow with generations of love carrying echoes of songs of yesteryear. They have witnessed many wondrous stories and countless colorful stories. Many stories are uplifting, describing the peaceful green valleys and mountainsides and rugged brown valleys. Others are narratives of overcoming obstacles in life, love lost, and love gained. They all happened at times amongst the snow-white mountain tops and during the stormy black nights of hardship and despair, and they all revealed the spirit of music in the souls of the people.

When hearing oral traditions told to me by older Black folks while I was growing up, I always was able to identify somehow with the strife and pain of their existence in slavery–learning in one-room schoolhouses, existing on an Indian reservation, and, yes, being sold and separated from their families. My life seemed in ways to parallel their lives as we were not afforded many civil rights during our childhood. I was intrigued by my ancestors' lives, stories, music, and culture, especially as I learned of the racial injustices they experienced during slavery. Why was the art of music and storytelling as important to these people as it is to me? The urge to understand more about my family's history overcame me even a young boy, and continued to plague my soul as their stories embraced me and my narrative unfolded.

What were the origins of my people? Some were born in these mountains, and some sought these mountains. Many Black families left the South, relocating North, after the Civil War, but many families stayed. Some came to East Tennessee for economic reasons, others to escape the oppression of the post-slavery segregation of the Deep South. Some came to escape the law; many came simply for hope and survival. They came from Scotland, from France, from Africa. They settled in these beautiful mountains of East Tennessee.

Throughout this narrative, I introduce some elders of my lineage telling their stories and singing their songs, weaving a mosaic of love for me and my heritage. I say "love" because I could not have existed without the impact of their stories on our culture and society—their struggles, triumphs, sadness, and hope for a better day. These are their stories and part of my song.

CHAPTER 2

Understanding the African Culture of My Ancestry

If a race has no history, it has no worthwhile tradition; it becomes a negligible factor in the thoughts of the world and stands in danger of being exterminated.

—Dr. Carter Godwin Woodson, 1926

HISTORY RECORDS THAT BLACKS, TAKEN from the western coast of Africa, arrived in Jamestown, Virginia, in 1619–four hundred years ago. Some historians purport that the first Africans taken from the Ivory Coast, or the slave coast, were indentured servants. It is this group that marked the beginning of slavery in the United States. However, most modern scholars disagree. Indentured servitude was essentially contractual labor that lasted for a set period of time to pay off debts or to serve for crimes committed–typically about five to ten years. The fact is that "chattel slavery", whereby people became the personal property of the owner, was quite different. People who were indentured servants could still freely marry, had civil rights, could own land, had homes, and were able to stay around their families. Chattel slavery was unlike anything that had preceded it in the history of the New World because there was a blatant denial of humanity in servitude that previously had not existed. The difference was that African people were viewed as lower than animals: They had no rights. Like cattle and other private property, they were bred, split from their families, whipped freely, could be abused or even killed, all with no repercussions.

While indentured servitude mostly happened to poor and vulnerable people, it was not widespread. It was not about subjugating an entire race of people into a permanent class of free labor. For example, children born to indentured servants were not the property of the people for whom their parents served. The masters had no claim to them in the same way they would if a slave bore children.

In 1789, Olaudah Equiano, one of the first Africans to write a book in English, described the area from which my ancestors descended:

> *The part of Africa, known by the name of Guinea, to which the*
> *trade for slaves is carried on, extends along the coast about*
> *3400 miles, from Senegal to Angola, and includes a variety*
> *of kingdoms* (Equiano, 1789, p.6).

Religion was a significant part of that region's value system. Religious rituals celebrated birth, puberty, marriage, death, harvest, famine, and life itself. Music, drama, and dance were expressive elements of these celebrations. These art forms were woven into the language and customs of all Africans. The value could only increase in a hostile land. A statement by Equiano reveals how Africans themselves regarded these arts:

> *We are almost a nation of dancers, musicians, and poets.*
> *Thus, every great event. . .is celebrated in public dances*
> *which are accompanied by songs and music suited for*
> *the occasion (p.8).*

In his diary, John Atkins, a British surgeon and slaver, gave a similar testimony to the importance of music in the lives of the African people:

> *Dancing is the Diversion of their Evenings, Men and Women make a Ring in an open part of the Town, and one at a time shows (sic) his Skill in antick (sic) motions and Gestulation (sic), yet with a great deal of Agility, the company making the Musick (sic) by clapping their hands together during the time, Helped by the louder nois (sic) of two or three Drums made up of a hollowed piece of tree (Atkins, 1735, p. 53).*

Like religion, music played a vital role in the lives of all Western and New World Africans. Unlike the "art music" of Europe, the music of the Black culture of West Africa was not a separate autonomous domain. Historian Tilford Brooks stated, "African music has no separate function, but rather is an aspect of social, political, economic and religious life" (Brooks, 1984, p.28).

Afro-American contributions to American culture have been significant. Even slavery produced many skilled Black professionals, including doctors, politicians, soldiers, scientists, educators, ministers, journalists, and musicians. Of these, the musicians left the most unique and indelible imprint upon America. Their art forms were as varied as the musicians themselves, but none was more significant than nor as enduring as the spiritual music.

CHAPTER 3:

The Andersons: Their Story, Their Song

Steal Away. Steal Away.

Steal Away to Jesus.

Steal Away. Steal Away home.

I ain't got long to stay here.

My lord, my lord, he calls me.

He calls me by the thunder.

The trumpet sounds within my soul

I ain't got long to stay here.

—*"Steal Away," New World Spirituals 1619-2019*

Anna Belle Broyles, Maternal Great-Aunt: Her Story

Our family, the Andersons, had our beginnings in Farmington, Georgia. My grandfather Jeff, born around 1847, and grandmother, Adeline, born around 1851, lived on a plantation as slaves in Farmington in Clarke County, Georgia. They had ten children, and both died at an old age. We all had a great big fireplace where all of us children would sit around as Granny and Papaw would tell us about living as slaves and how White folks treated them back then.

The Master, well, he would not allow them to do as they please. And if they got talking bad about the Master, well, they got beat bad by the overseer. Back then, when my grandparents were slaves, they were not allowed to pray, so they would slip away to pray. The slave masters always had a preacher for them to tell them, 'Obey your Master' and 'Don't kill and steal.' They preached on things that they wanted them to hear. Later, they learned of the heroes in the Bible, like Moses, which gave them a sense of freedom in the afterlife. The Master wouldn't allow them to communicate with each other on the neighboring plantations, so they would call back and forth and sing. These shouts and screams were their way of communicating. He said they sang praises to the Lord in the cotton fields. The overseer would allow them to sing because they got more work done. The slaves used to sing to lift their spirits while working the fields. On the plantation in the evenings, they believed in having a good time singing and dancing by the fire, but they favored the religious kind of singing. They always believed in a Promised Land, a land of freedom. I still get despondent sometimes, thinking how bad off they were living back then.

My grandfather Jeff was a profoundly religious man. Sometimes when he prayed, he walked on his knees and looked like he was talking to the Lord. My grandmother was a devout Christian as well. Her long longstanding request was that she not be taken to a funeral home when she died. We honored her right, and the older folks laid her out on some planks and placing a saucer of salt on her chest. Some say the salt helps the dead body remain, away from some rodents and a few other animals in the habit of coming around and digging the body up after burial. We all stayed up during the night singing spirituals and praying. The next day she was taken to the cemetery to be buried (A. Broyles, personal communication,1986).

Great-Aunt Anna Belle – Moving to Greeneville, Tennessee

In the 1920s, the boll weevil, destroying many of the cotton crops in Georgia, drove people away from the south. The times were happy for us but sad at the same time. Reverend Early, a Methodist Circuit Rider minister from Farmington, went to Tennessee and later asked my father Earl to join him in Greeneville. Papa went when he saved enough money to send for us. Just about everyone living around us was doing the same thing, leaving. Mr. Caleb Jordan and his wife, Walt Smith's Mamma and Papa came. When we got there, we met Walt Scott and his family from North Carolina.

The hardest part was leaving our family behind in Georgia. Papa shipped most of our belongings, and Mama and us kids rode the train. Being that we had to ride in the colored section, we didn't have the best accommodations. Mama had it worse because she had to deal with all of us kids.

I remember the trip as though it was yesterday. We had to bring our food. I remember riding the train through Atlanta. It was the most prominent place that I had ever seen. The trip was so long that I thought we would never get there. Mama would tell us stories when we kids got fussy, just like with Granny and Papaw around the fireplace. As soon as she would start the storytelling, we would settle down and get quiet and listen. Those stories were essential to us. It was almost like they were stories right out of a storybook, except they were about our own family (A. Broyles, personal communication, 1986).

James Jordan, the son of Caleb Jordan, added his memories about how our families traveled from Farmington to settle in Greeneville. His father Caleb and my great-grandfather Earl Anderson traveled to Tennessee by hitching a ride on a freight train – a dangerous but low-cost way to travel. The money they saved by "hobo-ing" and the money they saved from their jobs enabled them to transport their families to their new home (J. Jordan, personal communication, 2021).

CHAPTER 4:

The Storys: Their Story, Their Song

Maternal Aunt Minnie Wimbish: Her Story

History records that the (Grier) aka Story family originated in Columbus, Georgia in the 1840s. My parents were McDaniel and Sophia Grier, and my dad had three sisters: Pinky, Sissy, and Katie Lou, and his brothers were Tom and McDaniel. Tom became a minister. My father worked the land, and my mother kept busy with the children and did odd jobs to make money for the family. He had a love for music and was also known for his tap-dancing skills. Sometimes harassed, the police would fire bullets at his feet just to watch him dance. When courting, he would tap dance to my mama's house and continue to dance until someone answered the door.

At the age of 4, I walked barefooted to church. We lived in turbulent times. Not only was America on the verge of World War I, but lynching was a form of killing of many African Americans.

He sold goat meat. This White man told him to take some fresh goat that we had just dressed inside his house. As he entered the kitchen, his wife was bathing, she screamed, and he ran. The Ku Klux Klan would come looking for him. Upon their arrival at the house, I didn't know the reason, so I helped. I searched under the bed and in the closet. The Klan caught him. It was sad seeing my father being driven away in a wagon. His brother helped him escape with the rope still around his neck.

They escaped Georgia and fled to the mountains of East Tennessee. They both hid at my cousin Henrietta's house near a Cherokee Indian reservation. He left my family behind in Columbus, Georgia and changed his last name to Story, and then started a new family in Washington College, Tennessee. There he met Geneva Gillespie from Limestone, Tennessee. Back then, there was no medical help for women after having many babies, so she became bedridden at a young age. She died at the age of forty-nine from complications from having her last child. Papa worked on the railroad to provide for his new family. By God's divine grace, my father escaped the terror of the South and it was some thirty years later before we saw each other again. We never lost connection after our reuniting (Staples, Kirby, and Wimbish, 2012, p. 16).

Aunt Minnie told the story of how the families reunited.

My brother Robert Grier served in the US Army when the segregation of the armed forces was part. In his unit, he met a gentleman named William Story. After knowing each other for several months, they began to talk about home and family. They became close friends. One evening as they were talking about home, a strange stillness overcame them. They stopped and were frozen in their tracks when they realized they were brothers from Tennessee and Georgia. They began our relationship as blood kin, bridging the gap of bringing John Henry's two families together.

I came to visit my father in East Tennessee as a young mother. I intended to visit my father, whom I had not seen for 30 years. When I arrived at the bus station, I saw this man. We made eye contact. I said to myself, and he certainly looks like my papa. Without changing words at all, your father, Walt, left. He caught a ride to Washington College and told my father, 'Daddy, Daddy, I saw your daughter.' My father asked, 'Why he didn't bring her back? That was prob- ably your sister.' So, your Daddy went back to the bus station, and she had left.

A lady had taken us to a boarding house that had rooms for young women. Your father found out where we were staying, and we rode to Washington College in a beat-up car to see papa. This story is so remarkable in that your father and I had a special bond without knowing that we had the same father, whom I had not seen in over 30 years (C. Anderson and C. Champion, personal communications, 1980).

CHAPTER 5:

"Lead Me, Guide Me"

Aunt Minnie's Story Continued

During the Civil Rights Movement, I was the lone woman who sat on the podium with Dr. Martin Luther King in 1958 at a rally in Columbus, Georgia. Dr. King spoke at the Prince Hall Masonic Temple. I introduced him to the crowd, for others were afraid to do so because they had bombings in Atlanta the prior week. We faced so many challenges and resistance because people believed King's perspectives on integration were dangerous during a time of segregation. But I wasn't scared.

But people who knew me well knew that I wasn't a college graduate, but they knew that I was a good speaker. When they heard that Dr. Martin Luther King was speaking, they wanted the best speaker that could get. They were look-ing for the one who had an education and had been to college, and all like that. So, they got Mrs. Baker from Eastern Star Chapter to speak. She called me; she said, 'They got me to speak on a program with Dr. Martin Luther King.' They said they wanted to get the best woman speaker on their program. She said that 'I know I can speak, but I can't beat your speaking.' She said, 'Now I'm going to recommend you and call them back and tell them I'm not coming.' That's what she did. She called them back and told them, 'If they didn't get their best speaker, it wouldn't be right.' So, she recommended me. I introduced Dr. Martin Luther King that evening. The podium King spoke at is still on stage at the Prince Hall Masonic Temple in Columbus, Georgia (Johnson, 2018).

Aunt Minnie's Baptismal

Wade in the water

Wade in the water, children,

Wade in the water

God's a-going to trouble the water

See that host all dressed in white

God's a-going to trouble the water

The leader looks like the Israelite

God's a-going to trouble the water

See that band all dressed in red

God's a-going to trouble the water

It looks like the band that Moses led

God's a-going to trouble the water

—"Wade in the Water," *New World Spirituals 1619-2019*

Let me tell you all about my first trip to Jerusalem for my baptism in the Jordan River. I put on my long dress, and I put a lace scarf just across my head, and I was on my way out in the hotel to get on the bus. There was a Black fellow who screamed and hollered, 'Here comes the queen, here comes the queen.' He thought I was a queen, and I said, 'I'm not a queen ' as I was getting on the bus.

The baptism in Jerusalem was something that I will never forget. Little ole preacher Reverend Lindsay was from Atlanta. He baptized me. When I met him in the water, I was much taller. He began preaching and saying his words before he carried me under the water. And when he brought me out of the water, they tell me that I went swimming up the Jordan. I don't even know how to swim. I went swimming up the Jordan ("M. Wimbish -100 Year Old Recites," 2015).

CHAPTER 6:

The Hamiltons: Their Story, Their Song

When Israel was in Egypt land,

Let My People Go!

Oppressed so hard they could not stand,

Let My People Go!

Go down Moses,

Way down in Egypt land.

Tell ol' Pharaoh to

Let My People Go!

—"Let My People Go," *New World Spirituals 1619-2019*

Aunt Josephine Eason and Cousin Mary Brownlow: Their Stories

Tabby Hancher, a slave born in 1800 in South Carolina, is the earliest known relative on the Hamilton side of the family, aka the Boggs family slave. The lineage is complicated. Tabby had one son, George Susong, born in 1815. George married Mary Sylvia Susong, who was born during slavery and was the property of the Andrew Susong family and the matriarch of the Hamilton family. George's second marriage was to Cynthia Boggs. Josephine Eason, my maternal great-aunt, and Mary Brownlow, my maternal third cousin, helped me piece together this history of the Hamiltons.

As far as history will record, they lived in rural Greene County, Tennessee. Mary Sylvia had four children, Mary, Greene, Henry, and Harry. Her union to George Allen brought forth four additional sons: George, Tom, Alfred, and Will. She named her daughter, Mary Susong, who married Benjamin Hamilton. Owned by the Susong family, Ben paid Andrew D. Susong $1200 for his bride. They were married on February 1, 1868.

Ben Hamilton, your great- great grandfather, was a slave from South Carolina but ended up in Richmond, Virginia. He was the trusted enslaved servant of Colonel Hampton. Grandpa didn't talk too much of the past. He would come to our house two or three times a week to care for us while mother worked. Being a farmer and excellent carpenter, he built his home on land, which the Susongs gave to Mary Susong. He would tell us stories. He would let us ride on his back or even allow us to sit on his belly. Grandpa had a long white beard, and sometimes we would comb it and braid it; he carried mail for the Confederacy from Richmond, Virginia, to Charleston, South Carolina.

After the Civil War, he settled here in these mountains. He changed his name to Hamilton. In the days of the War, the north banned the exchange of mail between the North and South in August 1861. He carried mail for the Confederacy through Union lines. He had to cross the rivers and mountains of the Appalachia, always taking the risk of being killed or captured. He remained a mail carrier until the Confederacy went down. His life was at times challenging as well as hazardous. Colonel Hampton explained that employing slaves as mail carriers were more trustworthy than that class of White men who will carry the mail with all that money and secrets.

During the Civil War, Greene County was a stopping point for my papa Ben. During his journeys, he met Michael Woods, who was a White mail carrier from Greene County. Papa would stop at his home for food and a fresh mule. Their families became very close, often raising crops and livestock together. They became lifelong friends even after the War. Father was an intelligent and trustworthy man.

Nine months after the Civil War had ended, papa met and married my grandmother, Mary Susong, a slave. After the Civil War, they married and had ten children. Papa died on July 15, 1932, at the age of 106. His lifelong friend, Michael, died on the same day. Papa died in the morning and Michael in the evening. My oldest brother, Greene, threw the first few shovels of dirt on the casket of Mr. Woods, then returned to the gravesite of my grandfather to bury him (J. Eason and M. Brownlow, personal communications, 1985).

The Hamilton/ Forby Connection

My fourth great-grandfather Joseph A. Swatsell (1800-1861) had one son with Marry, an enslaved servant born in South Carolina in 1832. William Swatsell, my third great-grandfather, was married to Mary E. Rite in 1857. William fathered three sons and five daughters.

His daughter Lillie (Clara Swatsell) Morrow (Freedman), my second great-grandmother, was categorized as mulatto, and was the illegitimate daughter of William Swatsell. Freedman was a name derived from being a "freed man"—a freedman or freedwoman being a formerly enslaved person released from slavery, usually by legal means. My second great-grandmother Clara married George W. Farbia (Forby), a man of French descent. My great-grandmother Media was the daughter of Clara and George. They all were considered mulattos in the 1920 U.S. Census. Media married Thomas Hamilton, my great-grandfather. Their son Carter, my grandfather, married Mary Alice Anderson Hamilton, my maternal grandmother (https://www. ancestry.com).

Ben Hamilton and George W. Forby, both my second great-grand-fathers, were close friends and were among the first group of Trustees at Pruitt Hill Episcopal Methodist Church, Greene County, Tennessee, founded in 1910.

CHAPTER 7:

"On a Hill Far Away"

MANY OF MY ANCESTORS LIE in repose in the cemetery on a hill at Pruitt Hill United Methodist Church. This beautiful garden of restful souls lies in the scenic mountains of East Tennessee. The hills and valleys are a reminder of God's creation: singing birds, whistling trees, horses, and cows feeding on the tall green grass on the hillsides, billowy white clouds that seem to be thrust against the fierce and spacious blue skies. The hills and valleys remind us that some people said that the mountains were like barriers keeping some people in and keeping others out. But in this beautiful landscape, the church itself has signified a welcoming table for all who came and continue to come in search of a welcome and new opportunities.

The mountains in the distance are like a backdrop to a stage play, a gentle guardian of the valley's beauty. As you drive up the hill, there is the comfort of knowing that you are home. So how did this church come about?

On January 7th, 1910, a group of men discussed having a building for worship and a school for their children. The distance to the church in town was too far from their homes, requiring them to travel by horse and wagon. With their faith in the Lord, they possessed a vision to organize Pruitt Hill Methodist Episcopal Church. The charter members were my

Great-Grandfather Thomas Hamilton, Mr. Thomas Carson, Mr. A Dixson, and Mr. George Forby.

The charter stated:

THIS INDENTURE made this 7th day of January A.D, between A.J. Bird and C.G. Bird, of Greene County, in the State of Tennessee, of the first part, and A. Dixson, Thomas Carson, Thomas Hamilton and George Forby ("Trustees") of the Pruitt Hill Methodist Episcopal church, of the second part, WITNESSETH. That the said parties of the first part, for and in consideration of the sum of One Dollar, cash in hand....

....To have and to hold the said premises to the said parties of the second part, A. Dixson, Thomas Carson, Thomas Hamilton and George Forby ("Trustees") and their successors in office, in trust for the uses and benefit of the membership of the Methodist Episcopal Church in the United States of America. Should said tract of land cease to be used for church purposes, it shall fall back to the said Bird Bros. (A.J. Bird and G.C. Bird) (Greene County Office of Deeds, 1910).

Pruitt Hill Methodist Episcopal Church became Pruitt Hill United Methodist Church following a series of church mergers. In 1939, The Methodist Episcopal Church South and The Methodist Episcopal Church, two White denominations, united to form the Methodist Church. At that time, Black pastors and churches belonged to a separate Central Jurisdiction. In 1968, the Methodist Church merged with the Black Evangelical United Brethren Church to become The United Methodist Church. As part of the plan, formal segregation ended and Pruitt Hill United Methodist Church received its current name.

The church was the center for both religious and social settings going back to the 1880s. During the summer months, folks who lived in towns near and far would come to the annual church homecoming or the August 8th weekend celebration to visit family. Still observed by many today, the 8th of August celebration was similar to our present-day observance of Juneteenth because it was a holiday commemorating when Andrew Johnson, the seventeenth President of the United States and local Greeneville resident, freed his slaves in 1863. It was a grand celebration.

An 1871 article from the Knoxville Chronicle depicted on the U.S. National Parks website (https://www.nps.gov/anjo/learn/historyculture/slaves.htm) shows that one of the earliest observances of August 8th was led by the 1st Officer of the Day, Sam Johnson, a former slave of President Johnson. A brass band joined a procession of citizens riding in carriages, on wagons, and on horseback while others walked in the parade to celebrate their freedom. A group of children marched in front of the procession carrying the American flag, a symbol of freedom. I have often wondered if Sam Johnson or President Johnson ever had conversations with my Great-Great-Grandfather Ben Hamilton, who served as a mail carrier for the Confederacy during the Civil War.

Always in their Sunday best at church, men would wear ties and jackets and fashionable hats. Women would wear their southern-style hats and bright, beautiful dresses, many of which were handmade. Those that could afford it would shop in a store in the city to buy dresses. Children ran around the grounds in their Sunday best; some played on the old school swing set while the teenagers visited outside in their cars.

During annual homecomings or funerals, the Fellowship Hall would have tables lined with the best cuisine of baked pies, cakes, green beans, corn, fried chicken, potato salad, brown beans, cornbread, and homemade rolls. Outside, one of the men would have RC Colas and Nehi grape and orange sodas, soaking in a massive tub of ice-cold water, which he would sell. At times we would pass the cold bottle of soda over our foreheads to get a bit of relief from the blistery hot summer sun. During the afternoon services, the congregation looked like a butterfly field as they fanned cool air with yellow fans given to them by local funeral homes. Sometimes, these fans flew across the room as some folks got caught up in the Holy Spirit or the singing or the preaching.

In the winter, after a deep snow, parishioners would make the trek up the hill, wearing boots, heavy coats, jackets, scarves, and hats to keep warm. Those who drove cars maneuvered up through the rough rocks and crevices of the gravel drive. Some were unsuccessful, and other congregants aided those drivers whose vehicles would get stuck or veer off track.

My grandfather, Carter Hamilton, and a group of trustees would arrive early to the church in the winters to ensure there was enough heat in the coal-burning stove. Other preparations included organizing the Sunday school materials and setting up communion on the first Sundays.

The schoolhouse located in front of the church had beautiful wooden floors and new desks where students learned basic lessons, including passages from the Bible. During the weekdays in winter, Arlan Bowers headed a team of young boys who would arrive at the schoolhouse early to collect kindling to start the fire in the old pot-bellied stove. They also would collect coal that was the source of heat throughout the day. The stove sat in the middle of the classroom. Its billowy, smoky soot at times settled on the freshly snow-covered ground. On snowy days students would make snowmen and even snow cream.

In the spring, school children would romp, frolic, and swing during recess. They had fun playing games on the playground and organizing baseball and softball games on a makeshift field.

Though the school was demolished in the 1960s, the remaining concrete steps of the old schoolhouse are a gentle reminder of where learning took place for these Black kids, where the more senior students helped instruct the younger ones. But most of all, the old steps are a reminder of a place and time where education was revered and relevant in serving this community in a challenging environment!

CHAPTER 8:

"Will the Circle Be Unbroken?"

GROWING UP IN GREENEVILLE, BLACKS were considered inferior as a socio-economic class; but our grandparents, parents, and other relatives ensured that we all had life necessities. As a child, I felt that I had a purpose in life. I seemed to know where I was going. I didn't know how I would get there, but I just had a feeling. I may not have known my exact destination or future, but I felt God had a purpose for my existence. I can't remember when music was not as much a part of me as breathing. I created a secret place to store my thoughts, a place to suppress my energies, and a place to meditate on life and especially ponder the music around me. The percussive clacking of the train as it rushed by, the sound of a high-pitched train whistle echoing from a distance in the night, the sounds of wind rustling through the trees seemed to attract me. These *musical* sounds became a part of my consciousness. I can vividly recall these imaginary musical memories from my childhood.

At times, my mind would seem like a kaleidoscope filled with scattered moments of déjà vu–having a deep feeling that I had experienced life in another place and time. Some would call it extrasensory perception; others would call it craziness. Some would say that I had a remarkable memory, while others would say that I was unique because I was born with a caul on my face. A caul is a piece of membrane that can cover a newborn's head and face. In folklore, a baby born with a caul would be the bearer of good luck and in mythology would provide protection from drowning.

I enjoyed playing outside with the other children, but at times I found it silly to be wasting time with aimless scuffling, tripping, and shoving. I often escaped from the obstacles that I experienced in my youth by retreating to the secret place I had created in my mind–a room upstairs in my head for deep contemplation–a place to identify with the past. This safe space allowed me to recognize and reflect on my forefathers' history, their trials and tribulations. How can we plan for what we wish to be if we do not fully understand who we are?

Mama and Daddy had five kids: Mary, the oldest, then me, my brother Don Anthony who died as an infant, Tony, and Douglas. If some family members were having a hard time, folks pitched in to aid those in need. Seemingly, mothers could stretch a meal to feed hundreds. On the weekends, one could pick up a fish sandwich or a cup of hash that missionary ladies would sell to raise money for the church. One could get a great Sunday meal if the county churches were having their annual homecoming celebrations where women would cook and bring their best meals to share with all who attended.

If you were below the poverty line for household income, you could pick up powdered milk, cheese and rice, and some meat in a can to have a decent meal. We hardly missed a meal. At our house, giant bags of puffed wheat and milk were a breakfast staple, but the most outstanding cuisine could be found at our grandparents' farm. They raised a garden every year, killed hogs for meat, raised chickens that would be prepared for a Sunday lunch, raised and canned vegetables for the winter, and made jams for the hot, warm biscuits served any time of the year. Breakfast staples at their house were homemade biscuits, country ham, jelly, fresh farm eggs, bacon, and milk, and occasionally a cup of coffee filled with fresh cream and sugar.

In preparation for the school year, we received some school clothes. Some were new, while others were "hand-me-downs" from older cousins and siblings. My mother purchased some clothing at Miss Elsie Gass's Thrift Store, a bit like the modern-day Goodwill. No matter the fashions, mothers in the neighborhood took pride in sending their kids to school clean, sometimes using lard or Vaseline to grease our ashy faces, elbows, and knees.

George Clem School was the only Black educational institution in the small town. As we entered the school each day, the halls were filled with laughter as big yellow buses unloaded kids from all over Greene County. The aroma of cafeteria food filled the narrow hallways. Food was prepared by some of the best cooks in Greeneville: Miss Lottie Blue, Miss Willie Horton, Miss Carris Robinson, and several other ladies in the community. They always wore their crisp white uniforms and hairnets. They all were kind ladies who took pride in serving their kids. The aroma of homemade rolls, meats, vegetables, and the desserts that we later would have for lunch made us very hungry as we entered the building. Milk breaks were extraordinary. For an occasional treat, we would get cinnamon toast soaked in butter or peanut butter sandwiches or an oatmeal cookie.

The senior high classes were held upstairs near the library, with adjoining home economics and science rooms. As first and second graders, it was frightening to go up the two-level staircase to the high school classrooms. Yet my sister Mary and I would make the trek upstairs daily to get our nickel for milk break money which our Grandmother Mary Alice would send by my mother's sisters, Aunts Barbara and Joyce.

Upon entering the senior high classroom, we would raise our hands in the air to address Miss Lottie Henry, the senior homeroom teacher. Her tall stature towered over our tiny bodies like a graceful gazelle. At the beginning of each school day, we would chant in unison to our aunts, *"Can we speak?"* Miss Lottie's response was, *"Can you?"* She prompted us to ask, *"May I speak?"* Later, I realized that she was instructing us on proper grammar and at the same time teaching lessons of gratitude and manners. She would always acknowledge our presence, *"Yes, you may speak."* By end of my first-grade year, I dreamed of having classes on the second floor with Miss Lottie! She was such a kind woman.

My first-grade classroom, the quintessential 1960s style educational space, was adequate for learning. Twenty tiny bodies were seated at small desks where we stored our writing tablets, pencils, glue, and lunch for those who brought it from home. Sometimes there was an occasional marble to trade during recess. Cat eyes were the favorites to trade.

Over the chalkboard were block letters with large and small capitalizations. Other bulletin boards would display numbers. Our reading books sported images of the rich-looking Caucasian children, Dick and Jane, and their dog, Spot, running and frolicking in the best attire and beautiful environment, so different from our lives. Our best book that our teachers read to us was *Little Black Sambo* about a dark-skinned Indian boy dressed in fine clothing chasing a tiger to make butter.

The front hallway was the gymnasium where we had physical education, some assemblies, and sports events.

Aunt Joyce and Aunt Barbara, my mother's siblings who were seniors when I was in the first grade and my sister Mary in the second grade, were more like older sisters than aunts. They would take me and my sister on many adventures. Going to downtown Greeneville on Saturdays was a huge treat. Other outings included going to The Grill on Davis Street, where all the high school kids would hang out, dance, socialize, and even sneak kisses in the booths. Mr. Charlie Mack, the owner, would always have the menu of fountain sodas, ice cream cones, stick candies, chewing gum, and sometimes chicken and fish sandwiches available for sale. The focal point of The Grill was the jukebox, which played popular 1960s tunes. Many customers, including my sister and I, would "cut a rug" to the swinging tunes. We did not dance to the slow songs, but they were our cue to sneak and watch the jukebox as the records magically changed.

My grandmother always suggested that we go along with our aunts so not to get into trouble. The streets on Saturdays were bustling with all types of stores. Woolworths was the primary store for shopping. During our downtown adventures, I could see past the moment and project places where I would go. I would seek answers to why we were privileged to have our own "colored only" water fountains, and was surprised to discover that it was clear water, not colored water like cherry-flavored Kool-Aid. During the summer we could go to movies at the Capitol Theater downtown with our own special entrance.

Even though we had grown up with seating restrictions at the movies, were served food in the back alleys of the drug stores, and not allowed admittance to downtown restaurants, I started to feel a bit liberated as I attended school. Why was sitting on the balcony at the movie theater, called "nigger-heaven," regarded as degradation. I could still find the joy of seeing a movie and hearing the music from a different perspective. Was sitting in the back of the bus so bad? I could see the interaction of the people seated in front of me. To my surprise, regardless of the water fountain signs, everyone drank the same water.

Once I recognized the degradation of these guidelines in the rulebook of racism, I began to recognize what could be achieved. My ah-ha moment became apparent. With hard work and perseverance, I could become a part of a bigger world. There was a new way of questioning rules–we could overcome the curses of the slavery of our great-great-grandparents. Through the civil rights movement, I could start to experience a new way of thinking for the future. I could enjoy this new freedom and obtain prosperity by embracing education.

CHAPTER 9:

"What a Friend We Have in Jesus"

DURING MY FOURTH-GRADE YEAR AT George Clem, our family moved to Johnson City, Tennessee. My father interviewed for a music job at St. Paul AME Zion Church on Melbourne Street. One Sunday evening, Mama dressed us in our best. My father gave his testimony and had us all in front of the church. I watched as his weathered hands played the hymn, "What a Friend We Have in Jesus." His gospel voice wailed throughout the congregation as my mama and her four kids tried to join in. He met with the church elders after the service. They refused to hire my father because they needed some-one who could read music. After I overheard Mama and Daddy discussing in anger why my father didn't get the job, I vowed somehow I would learn to read music. The next time I attended that church was when I played piano for a friend's wedding in 1976, ten years later. And I read the music!

Attending Dunbar Elementary School in Johnson City was exciting yet painful. We missed our friends and cousins in Greeneville. Even though the towns were only thirty minutes apart, it was a rarity that we visited. We had to walk to Dunbar Elementary each day. Our shortest route to school involved walking past North High School on Roan Street, an all-White school. Again, I observed that our education was vastly different from that of the White kids.

These kids were nicely dressed in shiny shoes, coats, and jackets and had new book suitcases and all kinds of new textbooks. They looked like "Dick and Jane," whom we read about in the first grade. Unlike these kids, we carried tattered and torn books wrapped in brown grocery bags to keep them from getting wet during inclement weather.

As we walked along the sidewalks in the mornings, we experienced the welcome wagon shouts of familiar expletives and epitaphs. Several White students found this situation humorous, and their faculty did nothing to rectify the disrespectful behavior. Some students blocked our passage, while others would allow us to walk right past them without being confrontational. Later, we would walk across to the other side of the street to defuse these encounters. One morning, a group of White students brought baskets of apples and oranges for our lunch. I wondered why some of those kids made us feel so bad while others were so kind.

Another morning, one of the Black children in our walking group had enough of the name-calling. He struck a White student. After this incident, the principal and local officials ordered us to take a different route to school. We were forbidden to walk the shortest distance to the school whether in rain, snow, or sunshine.

Dunbar Elementary School had an outstanding reputation. Music class was still my favorite class. Coming from a strong foundation of elementary school music at George Clem, I felt that moving to this new town was a blessing for my musical career. We moved next door to my fourth-grade music teacher at Dunbar Elementary, Mrs. Mildred Goins. Across the street were my parents' friends, the Carters, who had a massive piano in their front room, and also across the street was the all-Black high school, Langston High. My musical life was evolving. Mrs. Goins taught us how to read musical notation, how music was structured, and performance techniques. I could hear her playing the piano daily during the summers as we played hopscotch on the sidewalk. During lunch at Dunbar, the principal, Mrs. Owens, would not allow us to talk, but she played recordings of Frank Sinatra, Ella Fitzgerald, and some classical pieces. *No talking–all music.*

We lived on the corner of Elm Street. In the afternoons during the fall, the Langston High Band would rehearse on the pavement right across the street. My sister and I would peer through the wire fence as the band practiced their show. We were transported to another place and time as we watched the band director instruct. The drum major bent back making fancy dance moves and majorettes marched in synchronization with flashy moves and dance routines, while the band members played so masterfully on their instruments. Little did I know that one day I would become a *Leader of the Band*. Was this a foreshadowing of my destiny? I can still hear the band playing Al Hirt's tune, "Sugar Lips." At times we would march around the yard with me practicing my drum major moves, and my sister twirling a stick pretending that she was a majorette. We loved these days in Johnson City.

We moved back to Greeneville after only one year in Johnson City.

CHAPTER 10:

Summertime

MY SISTER AND I WOULD walk from the city to the country with our Aunt Joyce during many summers. Aunt Joyce acted as our sister, our mom, our teacher, and our friend. We would follow Aunt Joyce around like two ducklings following mama duck. We would have followed her to the moon and back.

The summers were hot, but we often walked barefoot on the hot tar-riddled pavement. We would walk to the rhythm of a drumbeat as our feet kept a quick cadence with Aunt Joyce and we tried to avoid getting badly burned. We would alternate walking on the pavement with walking on the grassy, rocky roadside areas to cool our soles. At times we would stop by a creek to cool our feet. We would feel the mud oozing through our toes as we waded in the water after a crisp summer rain. We were happy. We were walking from Greeneville to visit our grandparents on the farm.

Our grandparents lived as sharecroppers on the Byrd farm. Our morning chores when we stayed over through weekends included milking cattle, slopping the hogs, and feeding the chickens. We roamed the hills to shoo cattle back to the barn after grazing on the Byrd farm. We picked green beans, tomatoes, and blackberries for my grandmother to can or make mouth-watering pies and cookies. Other days we gathered apples for fresh pastries and apple butter.

Fall brought indescribable colors that rivaled an artists' palette in their magnificence. My sister and I gathered walnuts in the afternoons — some green and some ripe — cracked them and picked the fresh meat out of hulls with a bobby pin. This left our hands covered with a black, often tar-like substance. Hog killing time was enjoyable as we took turns stirring the hog fat in the big black kettle pot over an open fire to make lard, a staple for my grandmother's cooking.

During snowy winters, my grandmother's kitchen warmed the spirit and teased the appetite with the smell of cherry and cedar wood burning. She cooked southern cuisine consisting of country ham biscuits and gravy in the mornings while the coffee brewed. The coffee pot became an aromatic alarm clock signifying that it was time to get up for the day. Sometimes we would gather snow which our grandmother would mix with sugar and vanilla flavoring to make snow cream. We were country kids at heart.

My grandmother, Mary Alice, seemed to always be busy in the kitchen. The kitchen was the centerpiece of the home–her sanctuary–and the love and joy she put into her cooking showed that she loved preparing meals for her family and neighbors. Mamaw was a short round woman with smooth, silky hair framing her smooth dark brown face. Even in her calico house-dress and apron, an air of dignity always surrounded her. As she shuffled her feet and worked around the kitchen, she would whistle tunes. She had a partial denture that she removed daily. She had worn the denture since an accident that she and my grandfather had when they first married. A bridge had washed out, and their car overturned on her, knocking out several of her teeth. I always felt she thought that the denture was a badge of courage, commemorating her survival from the awful car accident that occurred when my mother was a newborn.

Later my grandparents bought a house and moved to the city of Greeneville on Pearl Street, an appropriate street name because my grandmother was a pearl, a jewel! This precious gem symbolized my grand-mother's love for all who lived in the neighborhood.

My grandparents lived in a different house, but there still was a certain warmth that was familiar. The aroma of freshly brewed coffee in the mornings, crisp country ham and biscuits, sugar cookies, and fried fish found their way from the country to the city kitchen. Again, the kitchen became my grandmother's sanctuary of hope, peace, love, and joy.

We spent time playing on the playground, swimming, and going to summer camp on hot, sweaty days. But no matter what we were doing, my sister and I had to arrive at our grandmother's house by 4:00 p.m. on Wednesdays. Why? We had to deliver the famous cookies that she had baked for the sick and shut-ins in the neighborhood. Afterwards, we attended a mid-week prayer service at Tate Chapel United Methodist Church.

At times my sister and I were a bit upset that we had to participate in church as nine- and ten-year-old kids while others were outside playing. My grandmother insisted, however, that we join in these mid-week prayer services. The room for prayer service was a side room of the church building and had wooden floors. The same six to eight ladies would sing and pray and testify to God's goodness. Pastor B.F. Johnson was always in attendance.

One evening our grandmother insisted that we pray. We told her that we didn't know what to say. She said, "You both know the Lord's Prayer?" We told her, "Yes." We later became more comfortable reciting the prayer each week. She was so proud because we were the only kids there. Rev. Johnson would always pray for us. His prayer was that we would become workers for the Lord in The United Methodist Church. He encouraged us to come every week. I thought that he just loved us delivering my grandmother's sugar cookies.

My grandmother was a churchgoer. She loved the Lord. As a child, one of my most memorable experiences in the church was with my grandmother at a revival service. During the service, the minister delivered a very high-energy sermon. People in the congregation were singing loudly, shouting, and yelling, "Amens!" My grandmother was an avid participant in what I thought at the time was madness. Once we got home, my sister and I asked why she was having a "fit" at church. She replied that she was shouting and giving thanks to Almighty God for all the beautiful things that He had provided for all of us: our food, our clothing, our shelter, our health, and the ability to see one more day of living and breathing. She reminded us that her great-grandparents had to sneak away to have church because it was not allowed in their time. She reminded us that worship is an essential part of our existence.

We were always excited to go up to Limestone in Washington County, Tennessee, to play with our cousins on my father's side. Their lifestyles seemed so much simpler than ours. My father would have to drive the car over a creek to follow the trail to Uncle Hubert and Aunt Lucille's house. My Aunt Lucille could stretch a meal to feed all of us kids even if it was nothing but biscuits and butter. I miss those days.

When we visited our cousins in Limestone, we learned how to run wildly and freely through the fields. My father Walt, Uncle Clayton, and Uncle Hubert would go seining for fish. They would sew burlap sacks together and attach them to chopped-off pine tree limbs to make netting (a seine). Then, they would walk along the sides of the creeks casting this contraption into the depths of the stream. Suddenly, tiny bluegills would come flapping out of the burlap netting. The men also would take a long thin steel rod with a curved hook on the pole's end and go turtle gigging for mud turtles. Walking along the creek banks, they would push the rod into the muddy banks of the trees' exposed roots and pull out these monstrous mud turtles. They would then throw their catch into a burlap sack.

The bounty of bluegill fish would be a feast for three families including eighteen kids. The cleaned bluegill fish with the heads still attached were rolled in cornmeal, placed into black cast-iron skillets filled with lard, and cooked over an open fire. Mud turtles were thrown into an aluminum tub of scalding hot water to pre-boil. The ladies would cut up the meat and roll pieces of turtle in cornmeal and fry this juicy meat. The turtle tasted like chicken. My uncle warned us never to touch the turtles' heads, saying, if we did, this amphibian would bite our fingers and not let them go until the sun would set.

Our cousins, Uncle Hubert's kids, would always have initiations for us city cousins, such as daring us to urinate on the electric fence or daring us to see how long we could hold onto the electric fence. Of course, we took their dares, and the electricity sent shocks throughout our skinny little bodies. These were days filled with family jokes, meals fit for kings, and family bonding. Usually, at the end of these gatherings, we would all sit around the fire and sing! Occasionally one of my uncles would bring out his special brew, and the singing got louder!

We spent many days playing with their kids, playing "truth or dare," eating red clay, picking blackberries, or raiding apples from Uncle George Snapp's apple tree. We all started our day by eating puffed wheat for breakfast. My aunts and my mother could surely stretch a meal. On Fridays we knew we were going to get a treat for dinner. Mama would make a huge batch of spaghetti with tomato sauce and hamburger meat served with a white bread loaf. The meal was marvelous.

Women during this time did everything to keep the family together. They worked day jobs, catered parties for the rich White folks, took in laundry, and worked for dinner parties at the country club. These had to be the most enterprising women. When times were hard, they worked harder.

CHAPTER 11:

Church Music

SOME LOCAL CHURCH MUSICIANS COULDN'T read musical notation during my youth, while others played classical and jazz idioms. On Sundays, I could not wait to hear the church's music, the choirs, the men's gospel quartets, and the rearranged White hymns that the piano players would masterfully interpret on the keys. I was always mesmerized hearing the haunting sounds of old spirituals born out of suffering and degradation. Some of them sounded hopeful. In others, release in death was the goal expressed. I couldn't wait for the sermons to end and the music to begin. I preferred the joyful, uplifting gospel songs where I found comfort and hope.

I loved the sounds of the church. Most of the churches in the community were old. Some had wooden floors that creaked when you walked and seemed to keep the beat of feet tapping to the rhythms of the music—booming like soldiers marching into battle. I would daydream and wonder where the music started and how it had evolved? I finally realized that the music reached back to where we were in the long gone past and then brought us home to the present. The shouts of "Amen" and "Hallelujah" echoed in worship, and gave comfort to my people as they had for more than two hundred years, even before my forefathers could read. By age ten, I could not have known the exact destination that my life would turn toward, but I knew that I was on a journey. I vowed to look upon life as my sense of direction led me. My life was being transformed with deep and powerful emotions that I could not describe. I could feel moments of laughter, and sometimes tears.

Little did I know that later in life, the *room upstairs* I had created in my head would recall memories that I had stored. That *room* contained the oral traditions and stories as told by my elders, the sights and sounds of coming of age, and the hate, love, creativity, and hope I was experiencing. My family migrated from other parts of the world to settle in these small, rural cities surrounded by majestic mountains in Tennessee. Family narratives transcended time and history to solidify my existence and give credence to my ancestors who had overcome the brutality, oppression, and prejudices of the South to eventually come to the table of brotherly love.

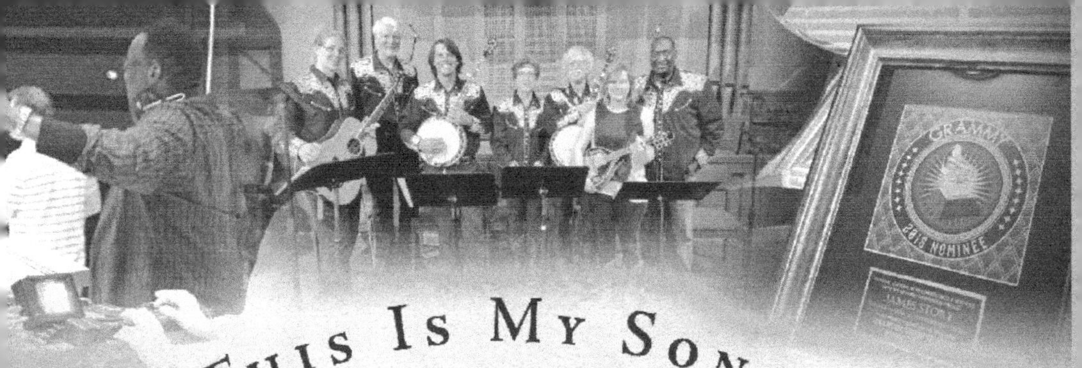
GRAMMY

This Is My Song

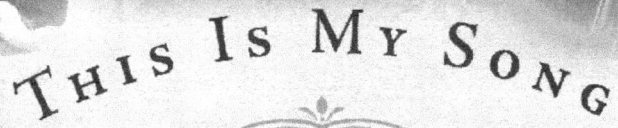

PART II

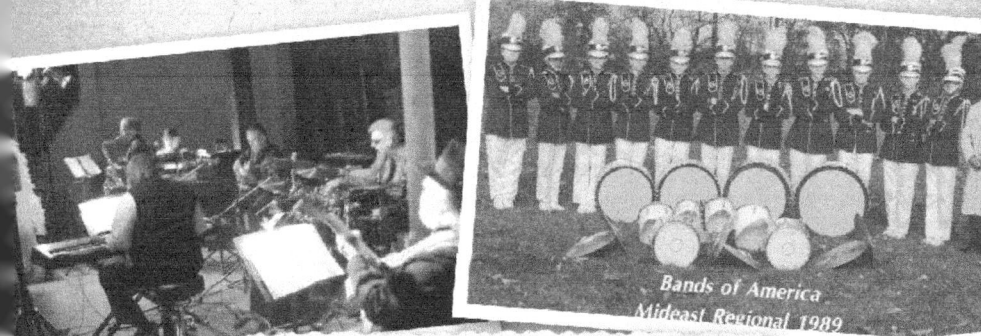

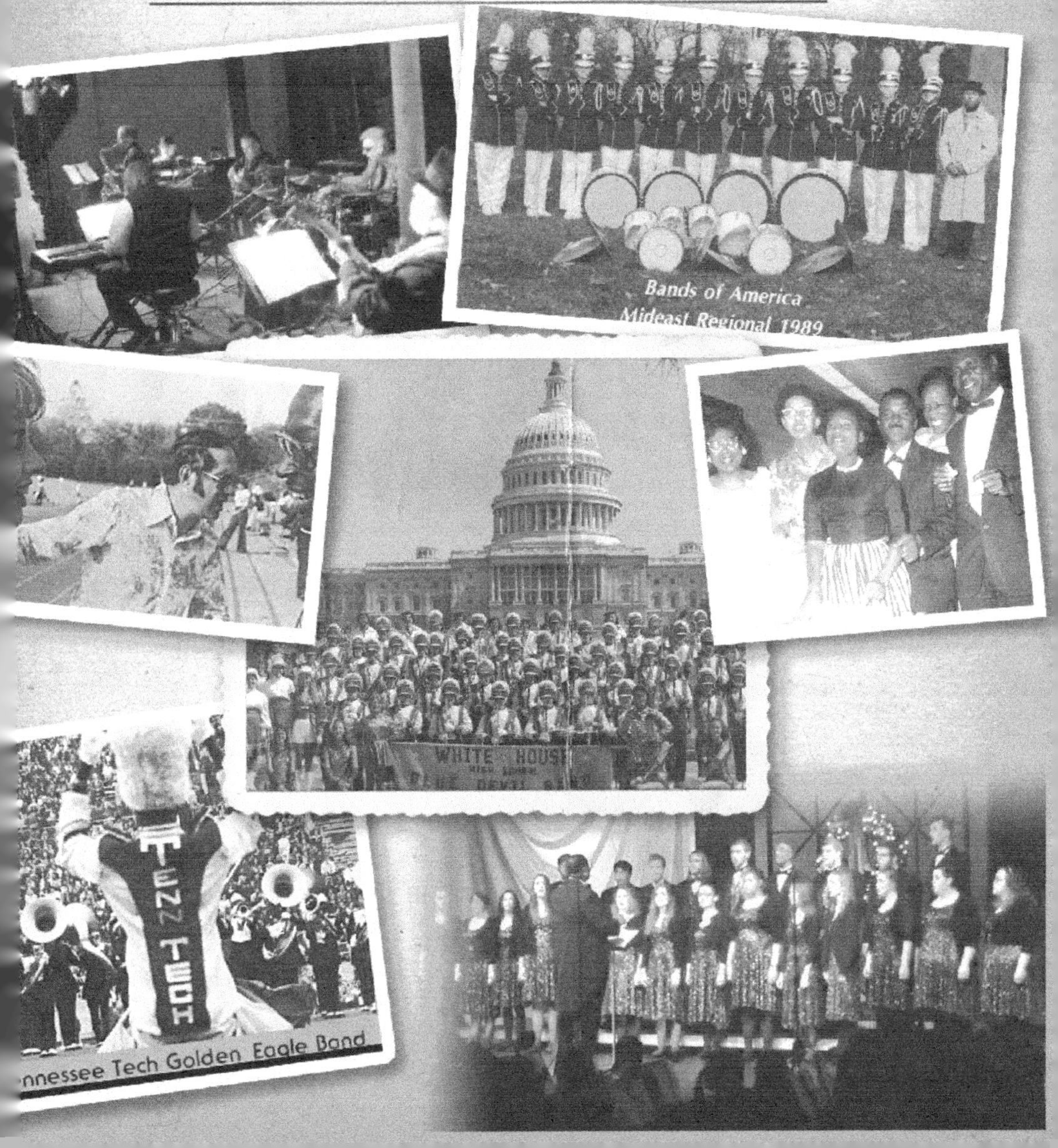
Bands of America
Mideast Regional 1989
WHITE HOUSE
TENN TECH
nnessee Tech Golden Eagle Band

CHAPTER 12:

My Musical Mentors: Their Stories, Their Songs

I WAS ALWAYS BAFFLED BY the many pianists that I heard during my childhood serving Black congregations. These were gifted pianists/church musicians in a small town nestled in the mountains of East Tennessee. I often wondered: How did they get here? How did they train?

Some trained under the tutelage of Mr. Roy C. Snapp, a classically trained musician of the early 1960s. Some were naturally gifted, while others just knew how to play through discovery learning. Were these some of the musical prodigies of African culture, or did they practice endless hours honing their craft? Noted educators Ms. Grayce Bradley and Ms. Georgia M. Farnsworth were icons of my childhood and youth. They both taught at George Clem School. Other pianists were poor Black kids coming from the farms. Some were domestics and cooks. Still others left Greeneville to continue their studies in music.

The church musicians played great hymns of faith, spirituals, and fiery gospel songs. Many musicians went unnoticed, playing for the moment, while others still play for church worship today. Many served Black church congregations graciously throughout their entire lives. One musician died while playing for an evening worship service. Some were paid, others were not. Some could not read musical notation; some had classical training. Some knew only one key. But all served masterfully with their blessed gifts.

The church musicians of my childhood had a significant impact on my musical career. How was Greeneville and Greene County so blessed with these artists that served? The list of includes:

Mrs. Treva Posey-Edmonds at Friendship Baptist Church

Mrs. MaryAnn Jordan-Jones at Memorial AME Zion Church

Mrs. Patricia Anderson-Elmore who served several local churches

Ms. Thelma Anderson

Mrs. Patty Sarden

Bennie Anderson, my great uncle

James W. Story, Sr., my father

Ms. Etta Scruggs, my first piano teacher

Aubrey Grady, my second piano teacher

Ms. Georgia M. Farnsworth

Ms. Grayce Bradley

Miss Elizabeth "Lib" Waggoner

Mrs. Beatrice Friend

Mrs. Sidney Barner

Mrs. Evelyn Elder

My Father Walt Story: His Story, His Song

Music in the Greeneville Community was alive. Music was a vital part of my childhood. Walt Story, my father, was a significant influence on my musical career. He was a great singer, played guitar, and played piano. He was musically gifted. My father played piano for Pruitt Hill UMC and other churches in the county and Johnson City. All my dad's sisters and brothers could either sing or play a musical instrument. My father and several local men would occasionally practice their singing parts and harmonies at our house. I was always mesmerized by how well they would voice the intricate and moving vocal parts.

I always knew when they had an upcoming concert because I would help my father process his hair. In the first half of the 1960s, many African American men processed their hair by applying a lye relaxer solution on their scalps that burned like hell. He would leave this homemade gook on his hair until he could not take the pain any longer, then I would set his hair into a slick style. After that, he would put on a Suzy cap. The Suzy was made from my mom's worn-out nylon hosiery.

Okay, think–*The Five Heartbeats!* Yes, *Gospel Rock Stars!* These men would sing fiery gospel songs at various churches on Sunday afternoons. They would do a morning radio show on WGRV and local stations as a warmup to what they would do during Sunday afternoon concerts at various churches. Uncle "Boots" Henry Anderson had a big booming bass voice. His voice could resonate so ferociously that the wooden floors of the tiny country churches would vibrate. My dad would sing and play guitar while others would sing in perfect harmony the songs of the "Five Blind Boys of Alabama."

My Aunt Margaret and several other ladies would always send their requests for the group to sing their favorite songs. Aunt Margaret's favorite was Jimmy Davis singing, "Sending Up My Timber." The ladies would scream and shout like they were at a rock concert. Aunt Margaret *loved her some good singing.* There were several gospel groups around during the time. Many Sunday singings were like fashion shows with coordinated coats, shirts, ties, and jackets worn by the performers. The winner of the day would be the singers who received the greatest response from the number of women who would scream, shout, and faint. Well, guess where my mama and daddy met!

One of my most memorable father-son moments was when I was in the first grade. In my *Boys' Life Magazine*, I found a card to order twelve albums for twelve cents. I joined the Columbia Record Club. Once my father found out that I had joined the club, I knew I would get the scolding of my life when the records came with a bill. My mother interceded, exclaiming that this was a way of getting more music in the house. After that, we heard many recordings of Brook Benton and Lou Rawls ordered by my mom. My tastes were different. I had ordered The Supremes, Mary Poppins, The Temptations, Little Stevie Wonder-Fingertip's Part 1, and the Jackson 5.

My Grandfather John Henry Story: His Story, His Song

My father was not the only offspring of John Henry Story to exhibit musical talents. My paternal grandfather's descendants have made an indelible mark on modern music history. In addition to pursuing careers in acting and education, some have exceled as music producers and recording artists. Others are composers, disc jockeys, and radio personalities across the United States.

My brother Tony carries on the tradition of singing in gospel quartets. He travels and performs with various groups throughout East Tennessee.

Ms. Elizabeth Waggoner: Her Story, Her Song

I was eight years old when my family lived on Robinson Street next door to Footie Robinson and Elizabeth Waggoner. Miss Waggoner, called "Lib" by her friends, was a beautiful lady with fair yellow skin and long, flowing black hair. She could play piano beautifully and sing so majestically. Her voice was as pure as silk, dispersing otherworldly sounds and vocalizations into the air around her. She could draw listeners into a realm of pure beauty and joy.

I would visit and sit with Miss Waggoner daily. She was bedridden most of the time, but during my visits I would assist her as she would drag her feeble body out of bed to the piano bench for my special concert. Music connected us.

She had a black choir robe hanging on her closet door that she used whenever she played at local churches. One day I asked her if I could try on the robe. She agreed, and, thereafter, every time I visited, I would put on my magical choir robe and conduct her playing and singing. She had the voice of an angel with her beautiful yet fiery gospel tones. She was my Muse!

Ms. Etta Scruggs, My First Piano Teacher: Her Story, Her Song

My Grandmother Mary Alice always knew that I loved music. She saw what joy music brought me. She saw how I would gravitate to the piano at church when we arrived early on Sundays. She recognized my gift for music. She then realized that she wanted to encourage me to go deeper into music and began to invest in me honing my skills as a musician.

At the age of thirteen, I would take a weekly lesson with Mrs. Etta Scruggs. My grandmother would give me a quarter to go down in the "holler" to take piano lessons from Miss Etta, a kind and gentle woman. Quarters were hard to come by in those days for my grandmother. This was a time when domestics would be paid only a dollar a day for cooking and cleaning in the White establishments' homes. She worked for Dr. Laughlin, a local physician.

Miss Etta lived with her son, Charleston. The old, out-of-tune piano sat majestically on the slanted wooden floor of her bedroom. Lying haphazardly on the piano were many old hymn books and sheets of music, many tattered and torn. She refused to teach me anything but hymns out of the brown United Methodist Cokesbury Hymnal. Her favorite selection was "Jesus, Lover of My Soul." I could always see her swell with pride as she beat her weathered hand on the instrument to keep rhythm as I struggled to play—at times successfully. She would sing the song in irregular rhythms at times, closing her eyes as though she was in deep meditation and worship.

Her son often would entertain men in the neighborhood with an occasional "social hour" in the front room during some of my morning lessons. One morning while waiting for my assignment to begin, someone yelled, "Story, play some of that Boogie-Woogie music." I tried playing the typical boogie-woogie chordal progression. Suddenly, Miss Etta came running into the room and insisted that I stop immediately. She exclaimed, "Don't ever play that kind of music in my presence again. That is the Devil's music!" So, I continued to play "Jesus, Lover of My Soul," until I couldn't take it any longer. I guess that was my first time to play church music in a juke joint!

Uncle Bennie Anderson: His Story, His Song

One of my fondest memories involves Great-Uncle Bennie Anderson, my Grandmother Mary Alice Hamilton's brother. Uncle Bennie was known to pick up the neighborhood children and his kids and form a children's choir at Friendship Baptist Church. He had an old car, named Hully, that would creep and smoke as several of my cousins and his kids set off on Sunday morning.

He and Aunt Helen lived on Cedar Street. One afternoon while we were visiting, he took me and my sister to his piano room, where we watched his huge hands glide blissfully over the weathered piano keys. He began to sing, "Nothing but the Blood of Jesus." How that room did reverberate with his smooth, silky but boisterous tones that seemed to consume the space! I was mesmerized by his skills. Kids on the next street would stop playing as his sound would fill the neighborhood when he practiced his church music. I later heard through his son, George, that Uncle Bennie was diagnosed with an eye ailment, and doctors told him he was going blind. That did not stop Uncle Ben. He practiced at nighttime with a dimly lit candle, so if he were to go blind, he still could play skillfully on the keys.

Uncle Bennie got a job as an elevator operator at the First National Bank. He was a great piano player who impacted many lives, for he played piano at two or three churches every weekend for years. He taught himself to play. My Great-Aunt Anna Belle told me this story:

> One evening at a church service, he sure got the congregation singing that night. The choir ain't never sounded any better. The church was packed and incredibly hot. It was one of the best services that I attended; the next thing we knew, somebody yelled, "What's wrong with him?" The music stopped, and the entire church got still. It was Bennie. He fell off the piano bench. Everybody crowded around him, some of them carried him out of the church and to the hospital. By the time they got him there; he was gone. I always heard him say that he wanted to die playing the piano and he did; and boy, did he play that night! (A. Broyles, personal communication, 1986).

Miss Grayce Bradley: Her Story, Her Song

My elementary school music education started with Miss Grayce Bradley, my first-grade teacher at George Clem School. She was also the organist and a music director at Jones Memorial AME Church. She was a motivator, a dedicated master teacher.

The Negro Women's Civic Club invited our class of first graders to present a program for their Annual Luncheon. Miss Bradley oversaw the program. She instructed us to cut and use construction paper to make our masks depicting various animals in the forest. We started rehearsals for a big stage production of the story of "Little Red Riding Hood." Wow! What fun: singing, dancing, and acting in costumes made by some of the parents. We were making our debut as performers!

For the luncheon, the women dressed in their finest clothing and wore matching hats and gloves. The tables were decorated with crisp, clean white tablecloths and perfect place settings, accompanied by proper cutlery and fresh floral arrangements.

Our performance was a success as the crowd showed appreciation for my music teacher and her troupe of jazz singers and dancers. This performance, my first stage production, became my introduction to jazz as Miss Bradley played a recording of Ella Fitzgerald's "A-Tisket-A- Tasket." After the recording stopped, we sang and danced wildly in our costumes as she continued to play her jazzy rendition of "A-Tisket-A-Tasket." What creativity!

Miss Bradley would invite the children in the community whom she felt had an aptitude for music to participate in various musical activities at Jones Memorial AME Church, including the children's choirs. She also served as an organist for the summer music enrichment program.

She encouraged various music students to sing and play our musical instruments during worship services and other social events in the community. She kept up with students who were in the music programs even after the school system changes that occurred with integration.

When I was about twelve, the summer between my seventh and eighth grade school years, Miss Bradley took the youth choir of Jones Memorial AME to sing for the church's conference in Abington, Virginia. She had assembled an ensemble of about fifteen young people to form the choir! We had a great time staying overnight in a hotel. "I Said I Wasn't Gonna Tell Nobody," a traditional gospel song made famous by the Joyful Voices of Inspiration, was my favorite song!

Treva Posey-Edmonds: Her Story, Her Song

After sixty years serving the Friendship Baptist Church, Mrs. Treva Posey-Edmonds reigns supreme as the longest serving musician in Greeneville's Black church history. She has played the piano faithfully and skillfully for weddings, funerals, and an untold number of community events. The hours she has spent preparing for events and the families she has touched are countless. Not only does she play the piano, she has continued to add her deep velvety alto voice to the many vocal ensembles she has played. I am proud to call her a friend.

Treva studied classically as a child because her mother insisted on proper training. As a youngster she received the highest rating of "superior" in competitions and festivals in the Tri-Cities area. She was only twelve or so years old when Rev. C.C. Mills, Sr., became pastor of Friendship Baptist Church and asked Treva to play her newly learned hymns from her hymnal for church services. She has played at Friendship Baptist ever since.

Upon graduating from high school, Treva's goal was to earn a degree in music, but life's road took a different turn and she became a young mother. The change in plans did not stop her, though, from instilling the same values taught to her and insisting on proper training and higher learning for her children, Dawana Gudger-Richardson and Lonnie Gudger, Jr., who both earned college degrees in music. Not only is she an accomplished musician, but her children Dawana and Lonnie also are accomplished musicians in their own right.

Treva has been an innovator in Greeneville's church music as she has boldly added drums, tambourines, guitars, the cabasa, and conga drums to musical presentations. She has taken choir gospel music to a new level.

Treva is a Greeneville treasure.

CHAPTER 13:

Integration - Unity in Action

GROWING UP, QUESTIONS OFTEN PLAGUED me about my existence and my role in this mixed-up society—a society that decreed a Black person was free but free only if he or she displayed an "across-the-tracks" attitude. The society of the Jim Crow South dictated we were subhuman and we were taught by our parents, grandparents, teachers, and ministers that we must overachieve just to be considered average. However, after schools were integrated, many White teachers accepted and accommodated the new Negro students who came to school.

The Greeneville City Schools system tried to comply with integration by placing teachers into new situations. Both Black and White teachers would teach a new diversified student body within the city—students who brought various levels of learning skills and students who would need to adapt to the town's new social structure. There were no standardized test results for students coming from a Black learning environment. This system of integration was being tried only 100 years after the end of slavery in America.

Would racial tensions be as prevalent as we saw reported on the evening news programs? Were there going to be problems with integrated restrooms or cafeteria issues with Blacks and Whites eating together? The questions seemed endless for both Black and White families.

Integration may have been easier for our small town since many county folks were agricultural; many farmers, both Black and White, had worked together on the farms. Seemingly, our integrated schools were not as contemptuous as we had heard about in other counties. Fresh on the minds of Greeneville residents were the horror stories of school bombings as close as Clinton High School in Anderson County in 1958.

Greeneville's integration plan was intentional. The teaching and learning strategy consisted of a city-wide initiative to assimilate Black students into a three-track system of teaching and learning: a college-bound track, a vocational path, and a general education track. Many Blacks were nervous about venturing into the new integration system. We had grown up seeing signs that read, "Colored Only," sitting in the balcony area of the segregated Capitol Theater, and being served ice cream from the Big Top Restaurant's outside window!

In retrospect, the Greeneville school system had a brilliant idea in integrating schools. They sent our new White teachers to visit our homes and meet with parents and students. The new teachers talked about how they were excited for us to come to their school. Additionally, the George Clem faculty also encouraged us to do well. In addition to Mr. John Jones, Mrs. Fannye Jones, Miss Georgia Farnsworth, Miss Lottie Henry, and other Black educators, one man comes to my mind who may have been an unsung hero of the transition! Mr. Gene Proffitt, a White band director who was teaching band at our school before integration, had won the trust of a few Black parents and the administration in Greeneville.

Mr. Proffitt had met with students and parents the previous year and started building common ground by bringing music into the mix! The reason for the meeting was to discuss purchasing individual instruments for my sister's class. They were the first group of students to have the opportunity to play in the band, and they were the last sixth-grade class that attended

George Clem! Miss Farnsworth encouraged that class and our fifth graders to participate in music when we enrolled at our new schools. I remember seeing both Miss Farnsworth and Mr. Proffitt working as a team as they taught these youngsters! I would occasionally peer through the door to listen to their rehearsals.

I started band as a sixth grader at Andrew Johnson Elementary. In the spring, one of the most remarkable things happened. A spring band concert, held at the Greeneville Junior High gymnasium, featured a combined band of all the sixth graders from across the city and the Junior High Band. Why was this important? Mr. Proffitt showed school officials and both Black and White parents that music had no color barriers. The integrated audience was comprised of a diverse mixture of parents and community leaders who experienced music's power. Through the magical conducting hands of Mr. Proffitt and Junior High director Danny Treadway, the band concert was a key step toward bringing us all together; and I was part of it.

CHAPTER 14:

"Pass Me Not O Gentle Savior"

One day, in the band room, I overheard a few young women of color, who I like to think were my friends, talk about the good old days at George Clem. The conversation was not hateful, somewhat reminiscent about the old days when so and so was the homecoming queen and so and so was a beloved cheerleader and how so and so was Mr. and Miss George Clem. That's when I, a young miss White girl, realized that Integration had taken all that away from them. Pretty sure we White folks thought Integration must be a great thing for the Negroes! They weren't resentful but just reminiscent. It made me so sad. When I was a cheerleader, I resolved a couple of years to do my best to help elect our first Black cheerleader in GHS history. Never was there ever a more deserving person than Denise Carter. And I was never prouder of my hometown when she was elected. However, I will never forget hearing those conversations—an aspect of Integration we Whites never fathomed what they lost (F. Richards, Facebook conversation, 2019).

What did George Clem School and the Black community give up when faced with the new federal laws of integration? They gave up community, identity, and pride. Would there be no more "all Black" emphasis, a lost sense of cultural fulfillment? We were now part of the White world where our moms and grandmothers continued to cook, clean, and babysit our new classmates' families, where our fathers still struggled to find decent jobs, and where specific rules of the Jim Crow South were gentle reminders to keep us in our place.

Integration had its problems, and systemic racism still existed on all levels of the human spectrum. However, back then, with the onset of integration, there was one saving grace. The Greeneville City Schools, with faculties representing both races, made integration work by believing in the educators during this time. They thought equal access to education was the key to a successful transition.

The last yearbook edition from George Clem School was in 1961. There are pictures of championship sports teams in the album, a drama club, a student council, a glee club, class superlatives, and other activities for grades one through twelve. The yearbook showed a community of students, parents, and teachers proud of their school, culture, and heritage! Black students came from all over Greeneville and Greene County to attend! The book included pictures of a proud community of musical activities, a chemistry club, and a yearbook staff. All photos seemed to radiate a sense of pride. There was a Homecoming Queen and the Dairy Bowl Queen, men's and women's sports teams, basketball, football, and baseball. Now all were gone.

I saw many of my aunts and cousins participate in the student council, the yearbook staff, men's and women's basketball teams, cheerleading, and home economic classes. They all had a sense of community and pride, for they were the George Clem Wolverines. The class portraits were full of hopes and dreams. Many students shaped by George Clem became successful businesspeople, sports stars, lawyers, preachers, and teachers.

CHAPTER 15:

"This Little Light of Mine"

By the time I attended Greeneville Junior High, the plan for integration had worked like clockwork. The downside was that Black students had been assigned to and adjusted through a tracking system used to identify the best and worst learners. Life became structured for all of us. A new curriculum concentrated on reading, mathematics, science, physical education, and music or art. Greeneville's junior high school was one of the first schools in upper East Tennessee designed "in the round." It was the brainchild of Dr. Robert L. McElrath, superintendent of Greeneville Schools, who was later appointed Commissioner of Education during Lamar Alexander's term as Governor of Tennessee. In 1967, the school opened its doors and drew national attention as an innovative junior high school.

The school's physical design and curriculum departed drastically from the traditional junior high. The school's architectural design entailed a circular structure with the library as the building's central focus. New to the world of education at that time were open classrooms and team teaching. Classrooms in curriculum suites included the math area, science area, language arts area, and history area. Partitions dividing the classrooms were occasionally opened for several teachers to do collaborative teaching.

The library filled with books and encyclopedias was the showcase of this newly designed building. Reading material included *The Weekly Reader* and, at times, *Boys' Life* magazine! Our previous schools never had such access to the multitude of reading material, but something was missing. Books for elementary school students were mostly devoid of African American contributions to history or celebrity. Our reading books pictured only Caucasian students, and featured few if any Black accomplishments. Where were the personalities and history of Black America? One had to wonder whether a part of the newly integrated plan was to not educate Black children about their past? Regardless, we were becoming desensitized to our own culture and estranged from the beautiful, happy family photos that had been introduced to us in the first grade at our all-Black school!

The band rehearsal room, located off to the gymnasium side with pull-out bleachers for sporting events and assemblies, was my hang-out area. A stage was a part of the gymnasium which various speakers could share. The band rehearsal hall had built-in circular risers, instructional boards, and storage lockers for wind instruments, percussion, and tubas.

The school was not without a social class structure. There were affluent kids whose parents worked for some of the manufacturing plants in Greeneville, and others who were upper-middle-class families to us. To me, it seemed that most of the White kids didn't have to want for much. Some of our grandmothers were domestics in Greeneville who cooked, cleaned, and raised some of these kids. Many of the White students' families were members of the prestigious Link Hill Country Club, which excluded any Black families unless you were a waitress or cook or landscape keeper. There were children of doctors and lawyers and the city's historical bourgeoise. Then there were the poor White kids, and finally Black kids who lived across the tracks on Railroad Street.

Band, as I have mentioned, blurred our class distinctions and brought us together for one common cause. We all were there to make music. We loved working with our teacher and loved the time to forget all our troubles by making music. In other classes, I seemed to struggle. With the lack of reading books, the lack of knowledge of necessary math skills, and the lack of knowledge of our government and how it operated, I was lost and had to study more and play catch-up at times. The civics class was a real eye-opener for me, for laws were changing. I realized I was part of the change but had no idea how Congress or political parties operated.

My thoughts were bombarded daily by the Civil Rights Movement as it seemed to be televised each night on the news. How was it possible that people in other states were being treated so poorly, sprayed with firehoses, bitten by German shepherd dogs, and harassed at lunch counters? The televised political speeches by Stokely Carmichael, Eldridge Cleaver, and other so-called Black militants seemed to foretell even more racial conflict. Why was such evil going on across our country, while the mountains seemed devoid of these scenarios? This was a period of racial unrest in our country. But in our small community, we tried to go to school and get along with our White counterparts.

A phrase spoken in a recent movie, *Colette* (2018), triggered a memory from my teenage years. Upon hearing the words "The hand that holds the pen writes history," I was transported to a bittersweet moment in time in my eighth-grade language arts class with Mrs. Bogel Smith. On that morning, she entered our classroom with a calm demeanor and announced, "Today, we are going to learn the process of diagramming sentences using various parts of speech." She drew a diagram on the board that included all parts of speech that we would cover, nouns and pronouns, subjects and verbs, adjectives, adverbs, and prepositions. After she had written this old hieroglyphic-like chart on the board, a sick feeling came over me. I had no earthly idea of what she had explained! She continued to explain the charting process. She asked for volunteers to go to the board to help write in the various parts of speech. It was one of those moments when all students would bow our heads as though we were attending a prayer meeting service, trying not to make eye contact with the teacher and hoping that she wouldn't call on us.

Why was I running late that day? Dang, my locker combination would not work. At least I had taken my seat before the bell rang. To my dismay, I had to sit right in front of Mrs. Smith's desk. She said, "James, come to the board." I began to shake in my shoes. As she handed me the chalk, she led me through the process with much patience and precise explanations. I felt that she had targeted me from day one since I was the only Black kid in the class. In my mind, I could hear my mama say, *James, you have to work twice as hard as the other kids just to be average in the classroom.* Was I being too sensitive to think that Mrs. Smith was picking on me? Was she trying to prove a point? I started to ponder various possibilities:

1) Was it to teach our class a new system of writing and communication?

2) Was it to make me feel comfortable in this new learning environment?

3) Was it to prove to the class there were no differences in teaching a diverse class with the same ultimate goal of grasping writing concepts?

4) Had she heard of what had happened to me earlier that day in science class and felt sorry for me?

I was successful in comprehending this new concept of diagramming sentences while standing in front of the entire class. No matter why, I knew that I wanted to become a teacher at that point in my life.

I left Mrs. Smith's class feeling accomplished, but earlier that day in our science class, I had not felt so accomplished. Miss Clemmons had presented a lecture on hereditary traits. She had given us the assignment the previous day to bring our baby pictures to her classroom. Today the photos would be placed on the board, and we would go down the line to identify each student from these baby pictures. She then exclaimed to me in front of the class, "James, you will not have to bring yours because we know who you are!" I was shocked, being the only Black kid in class. My classmates chuckled. I ignored this kind of joking, for it was a moment that would repeat itself throughout my life, the feelings of ridicule, prejudgments, and subtle humiliation.

At the end of the eighth grade, I could feel my destiny. Mrs. Smith had compassion. She kept me in her classroom during breaks to tutor me privately on my writing skills. She relocated my desk right next to hers! I became her helper. She asked me to come to special tutoring sessions after school and would take me home. She was so loving and kind. I was her project!

I treasured this learning environment; I could not wait to get to school each day. My teachers were great, including Miss Clemmons. After some years passed, I realized that her comments might have been unthoughtful at the time, but she was teaching in a new environment for students of color. Keep in mind, this was just year three of integration in Greene County.

By this time, music had overwhelmed my life! My band directors, Danny Treadway and Gene Proffitt, both inspired me musically every day. They presented music in a way that was fun, demanding, and beautiful. How could this music become so addictive? The band played a massive part in my love for going to school each day. It was fantastic to play with a large group of students who wanted to excel musically. It was also an opportunity to see other kids of color, being that I was the only Black kid in my academic classes, other than physical education.

CHAPTER 16:

"Sometimes I Feel Like a Motherless Child"

Sometimes I feel like a motherless child

Sometimes I feel like a motherless child

Sometimes I feel like a motherless child

A long way from home, a long way from home

Sometimes I feel like I'm almost done

Sometimes I feel like I'm almost done

Sometimes I feel like I'm almost done

And a long, long way from home, a long way from home.

—"Sometimes I Feel Like a Motherless Child," *New World Spirituals 1619-2019*

MY GRANDFATHER HAMILTON KNEW THAT education was the key to a better life. His prayer became a reality as all six of his children graduated from high school, and two of them attended college. Uncle Donald attended Tusculum College, a local Presbyterian school, for a few terms to play basketball. The youngest daughter, Aunt Barbara, attended Morristown College, in Morristown, Tennessee.

In the 1960s, many Black parents who could afford it were sending their graduates to northern colleges because they realized the need to further their students' education outside the Jim Crow South. Several students, affiliated with Tate Chapel United Methodist Church and Pruitt Hill United Methodist Church, were overtly recruited to go to Morristown College. My Aunt Barbara Mae Hamilton registered at Morristown College.

All my grandparents' schooling had been church related. The Pruitt Hill Community School had its ties to the Greeneville Methodist Episcopal Church (Negro). After the ninth grade, my mother and her younger siblings attended George Clem School through the twelfth grade. George Clem School had ties to the Black AME Church. All my mother's graduating class received the same grade point average, and they all had the opportunity to speak at their graduation. My mother did not attend college because my grandparents could not afford it at the time.

Visits to the campus at Morristown College to visit Aunt Barbara were inspiring. Aunt Joyce would take my sister and me to visit her sister on some Saturdays. Going to downtown Morristown was always a treat, even though we would have to get our burgers to go and eat in the alleyway. But the thirty-minute bus rides were exciting.

We loved looking at the pictures in the Morristown College yearbook. Students from all over the nation attended college there. My grandparents were proud of their daughter Barbara, who graduated from the school within two years. She wanted to become an elementary school teacher.

Aunt Barbara graduated from Morristown College in the spring of 1964. After returning home to Greeneville after her graduation; however, she started to have severe headaches. The headaches were so painful that they made her ill. After being admitted to the hospital, she was diagnosed with an inoperable brain tumor and passed August 3, 1964. She had just recently graduated from college and was only nineteen years old. I was in the fourth grade, and it was a sad time for all of us.

Somehow, I felt my grandparents never got over the loss of Aunt Barbara. From that time forward, my grandfather, who now had a daughter who had finished a two-year college degree, hoped and prayed to see all his children and grandchildren graduate from high school. However, for the next few decades, he never attended any of his grandchildren's graduation ceremonies. My guess is that it reminded him of the hurt and sorrow of losing his baby girl.

On a positive note, I inherited several things from Aunt Barbara's box of belongings that traveled with her between college and home. I found a music book, *Teaching Music for Elementary Teachers.* I had found a treasure. Little did I know when browsing through it then that the book would lay the foundation for my life. I believed this book was a treasure left to me, to provide hope and encouragement in some ethereal way. Was she passing along a musical baton for me to pursue my dream through her? Someway I have felt her spirit in my life, and this connection solidified my hopes, dreams, and aspirations to 1) graduate from college like my Aunt Barbara Mae Hamilton and 2) become a music teacher. I did both! I was Carter Hamilton's first grandchild to graduate from a four-year college plus to go on and receive my Master of Music Education degree.

Outside Greeneville, a storm was brewing in a place far removed from our quiet little town. Our country's movement for equal rights for Blacks was especially tumultuous in the South. Were we in Greenville protected from this wave that was sweeping across the country like a tsunami? We saw on the nightly news how the media were portraying the violence. No one in our educational system was talking about it. Were we being silenced by our ignorance? Were we happy with the choices of staying in our place in our small corner of the cosmos? But the assassination of Dr. Martin Luther King, Jr., April 4, 1968, in Memphis, Tennessee, sent shock waves that reverberated across the world.

Was integration bringing new hope and opportunity to Black Americans, or were students giving up their cultural heritage and diminishing their history? Were we forgetting our elders who had made this small south-ern city a dynamic community of civic pride, noted teachers of education, and religious leaders? One thing was noticeably missing: political clout. There were no Black aldermen or civic leaders representing the Black community. Political power seemed to come only from the religious institutions: the Methodist, Presbyterian, Baptist, and AME churches. Was that enough to give Blacks progressiveness in the newly integrated social and political system?

CHAPTER 17:

"How Firm a Foundation"

MUSIC HAD BECOME AS NATURAL to me as breathing. How fortunate was I? Greeneville High was my home away from home. The band activities, being part of the thespian troupe, and becoming active in clubs and organizations such as the student council and the French club, were giving me opportunities that I may not have experienced at a segregated school.

In my junior year, something unique happened. My high school principal, Dr. B. F. Griffin, chose me and another close Black friend, Cecil Clayton Mills, Jr., to represent Greeneville High in a weeklong workshop in Washington, D.C. It was an honor to attend The Presidential Classroom for Young Americans Conference which allowed youngsters from around the country to experience our government's activities in Washington. We met with our congressmen, toured the U. S. Capitol building, attended a play at the new Kennedy Center which had opened in 1971, and met students from as far away as Boston, New York, Hawaii, Philadelphia, and California.

In the summer of 1972, little did I know that I would be following in Mr. Proffitt's footsteps five years later. I was on an adventure. I was on my way to drum major camp at Middle Tennessee State University in Murfreesboro, Tennessee. I had been chosen through a competitive tryout to be the drum major of Greeneville High School. Before that, I was the drum major for my middle school band in the eighth grade under Mr. Treadway. How historical was this accomplishment for our town? I'm sure Mr. Proffitt experienced many sleepless nights wondering how the city would react to this change: A Black kid from across the tracks leading the noted Greeneville High Band. Was seven years after integration too soon for the town's White fathers to accept this Black kid leading the band? The shock may have been lessened by the fact that I had been the drum major in the ninth grade at Greeneville Junior High and had proven my potential.

Black students were making great strides in football, basketball, chorus, and academics. The school had selected the first Black cheerleader. Why not accomplishments in band? Remember, I received my first training in the fourth grade, the year we lived in Johnson City, watching the drum major at Langston High School as my sister and I peered through the fence to see the high stepping drum major and flashy majorettes.

After I auditioned and received the drum major post at the high school, Mr. Proffitt suggested I attend the A. R. Cassavant drum major camp at Middle Tennessee State University. My mother, grandparents, aunts, and Greeneville Band Boosters all aided in paying the week-long training camp expenses. My mom took me to the Trailways Bus Station in Greeneville, for my trip to Murfreesboro, Tennessee. Upon arrival at the bus station, I began to wonder about the colored section in which we used to sit. To my surprise, the sign was gone. But the shoeshine stand was still there as a gentle reminder of who we were.

My Great-Uncle Henry "Boots" Anderson, drove a regular route for Trailways Bus Lines from Greeneville to Knoxville, Tennessee. I felt proud riding the bus that day with him, for he let me sit on the front seat of the bus behind him. I felt like his co-pilot as I stared at the gadgets on the dashboard of the bus! It was my only time I got to spend one-on-one time with him in my life.

Great-Uncle Boots was a regular member of the gospel quartets in which my father sang. He gave me advice on how to stay safe on my trip. He advised me to keep my billfold in my front pocket while traveling and be careful in Middle Tennessee because some towns were not welcoming to Blacks, and above all to not leave the bus alone until I reached my destination.

When we arrived in Knoxville, Great-Uncle Boots' route ended. I felt alone but proud that I was going to a music camp on my own. All I knew was that I wanted to conduct a marching band like that drum major at Langston High School that I had watched when we lived in Johnson City. Marching around the yard leading the band to John Phillip Sousa's "Stars and Stripes" had excited me. I felt the music. I became the music!

Mr. Joe T. Smith, band director of the Middle Tennessee State University Blue Raider Band, greeted me upon my arrival at the bus station in Murfreesboro. Once on campus, a student counselor registered me and showed me to my dormitory room. It was a single room with a bed and desk. I unpacked my belongings and made my bed for the week. The first night we had to meet for a conference before dinner. At dinner, a group of White students invited me to sit with them, and I began to feel so much at ease. We all became friends for the week. I was spending my first week at a college. I knew then the keys of education were beginning to unlock doors to opportunity.

Mr. Smith introduced camp counselors to all camp participants, which consisted of approximately three hundred students from throughout the Southeast. Again, I was the only Black kid. I was no stranger to this situation, for it seemed to follow me from middle school through high school. Mr. Smith's students taught leadership lessons, how to march with authority, how to conduct a band, and how to be a music leader in our schools and in the communities. After the camp concluded, Mr. Smith drove me back to the bus station and waited until I boarded the bus back to Greeneville. This man made sure that I, out of all those students, had a safe arrival to and departure from his camp. Little did I know after meeting Mr. Smith, that twenty years later my own Gallatin High Band Marching Band would be making its mark as a finalist in the coveted MTSU Contest of Champions Marching Competition in 1986. I accepted the trophy after Gallatin was selected as a finalist by a group of well-known adjudicators. The man who picked up this little Black kid at the Murfreesboro bus station became another mentor in leading me closer to a dream for my life as a bandleader. He encouraged me and thousands of other music students during his thirty-six-year career at Middle Tennessee State University and beyond!

As I mentioned earlier, drum major camp was my first visit to an integrated college campus. I loved it! My love for music and leading the band was beginning to guide my life, my dreams and ultimately my path to my profession. This profession would give me confidence and leadership skills. I would learn how to overcome uncomfortable situations when dealing with race relations and how to be kind and cordial to strangers with a gentle smile, and I would achieve my goals knowing that I had inadequacies of learning and acceptance. Knowing my challenges made me work harder. I could still hear my mother saying, *you must work harder just to be average in this society.*

On my trip home from camp, I was proud to have experienced life on a college campus and having met kids from all over the Southeast who were great musicians and many who later became friends.

It was on my trip back to my hometown from the camp when I met him: "The Man on the Mountain." I sat with an older gentleman who to me had the appearance of an old Black slave. He talked the entire trip. He told me stories of his hard life. He finally asked me where I was going, and I told him that I had spent the week at a music camp at MTSU. He became silent for a moment. I looked at his weathered face, and I saw him crying. Were these tears of sadness or joy? I did not understand. He was surprised. He asked me if I had stayed on campus? I responded yes and in a dormitory room. He told me that my life would impact many by leading people to music and my life would be blessed. He started to reminisce about his hard life, took my hand, and prayed for me that I would give the gift of music to the world and always keep God first. I remember riding through the mountains as we overlooked Rockwood, and I found joy and comfort in the encouragement of "The Man on the Mountain."

The camp experience was exhilarating and made such a difference in my life. I was so motivated afterwards that I ran for Student Council President during my senior year and was elected. I became active in my Methodist Youth Fellowship group and was elected president of our district youth.

Later, Great-Uncle Boots continued to drive for the Greene Coach Bus Line. In 1984, Gallatin was going to play Germantown in the state football playoffs. As band director, I was rushing around to get the band ready for the road trip. Suddenly, one of the bus drivers came to the band room and demanded that I come outside. There he stood. My Great-Uncle Boots was one of the drivers! I sat on the front seat with him as he drove, as I did as a sixteen-year-old, reminiscing and talking of home. I felt safe with Great-Uncle Boots. It was a proud moment for him to see me as the leader of the band once more.

CHAPTER 18:

"On Eagle's Wings"

IN FALL 1972, MR. JAMES Winfree, the choral teacher at Greeneville High School, and Mr. Treadway, my junior high band director, arranged an audition for a clarinet scholarship at Tennessee Technological University. Mr. Proffitt wrote a letter of recommendation to the music department chairman. This audition would change my life. Receiving a music scholarship to Tennessee Tech in Cookeville, Tennessee, starting the fall of 1973, was a major step toward achieving the career of my dreams.

My Uncle Donald Hamilton and my mother loaded a truck to take me to Tennessee Tech for summer band camp as I began my freshman year. After checking into the dorm, my mom helped me set up the room and mandated that I call home regularly throughout my four years of college. While making my bed, she became so overcome with emotion that you would have thought someone had died. I could not understand why she cried all the way from Greeneville to Cookeville, and continued to cry. It was a bittersweet moment because I was so excited about getting away from home. This was an exciting time for a seventeen-year-old. My eighteenth birthday was not until December; thus, I was young to embark upon this journey. But my lessons in independence helped me cope with new situations, and I didn't find it challenging to meet and engage with new people. I was always a talker.

My first year at Tennessee Tech as a music major was terrific. Summer camp which preceded classes was a breeze. It was made better by having several classmates from Greeneville also attending Tech. That made my first-year transition from high school smooth.

I had a great support system, but pressure increased after classes started. The Tech curriculum was highly demanding: music education classes, music theory, ear training, music history, private lessons, marching band, wind ensemble, concert attendance, not counting our other academic requirements of English, math, and sciences.

The second year was briefly interrupted by pledging the Professional Music Fraternity Phi Mu Alpha, and being active at the Wesley Foundation. In the summers, I would work music camps in Ohio, assisting bands with their marching shows. I was well on my way to becoming a music education major.

Arriving at college in Cookeville, Tennessee, I became more aware of race. There had been no severe racial confrontations on campus, but going to an unknown town in a different part of the state was a bit unsettling. There were less than fifty Black students at Tennessee Tech my first year. Blacks were advised not to go to town by ourselves and to stay together. The music students and faculty accepted other students of color in the department; however, there were no Black instructors on the entire campus.

One particular incident made me feel uncomfortable. We had an American history class in a vast lecture room that held approximately fifty students. Being the only person of color was still the norm for me! I was not a stranger to these situations. One day in the lecture covering the Civil War, the professor referred to Blacks in the south as "nigras." I had never heard that word, but it was like a knife stabbing in my heart every time he spoke it. It sent chills up my spine.

After class, I stopped by the Professor's office and told him of my feelings when I heard the word. He stated that he had always referred to Negroes in that fashion. I told him times were changing, and Negroes preferred to be called "Black." He attested that to him "Black" sounded offensive as well.

BUT the next day, he referred to the slaves as Black folks. Not only did I ace his class, but I also was proud that barriers had begun to break down from a simple conversation and mutual understanding.

I worked hard for the grades, for I had no other choice but to succeed. There are so many stories to tell of my Tech life, but that could be another book in itself.

My best Tech tale, though, happened in conducting class while we were practicing a basic four-beat conducting pattern. Dr. James Wattenbarger, my conducting professor at Tennessee Tech, yelled at me in front of the entire class, "Eh Lawd, Jim Walter Story! Get off the podium. You will never be a conductor; you will be a drum major for the rest of your life." First, he is the only person in my life that I have allowed to call me Jim. I always have felt Jim was a slave name. Second, couldn't he have been more tactful? However, by the end of my senior year, Doc had selected me to conduct the Tennessee Tech Symphony Orchestra for the first Student Concerto Honors Concert. I was the first student listed on the program to perform that evening. Wow! I was conducting a full orchestra as they performed Beethoven's *Prometheus Overture*. That was a proud moment. I look back over my life. I was the first African American drum major for my middle school band, high school band, and two college years at Tennessee Tech. I guess Dr. "Jim" Wattenbarger was right: I will be a drum major for the rest of my life!

These words still resonate with me. The title "drum major," the band leader, echoes through my life. Since those college days, I have conducted honors choirs, high school bands, church choirs, Broadway musicals, orchestras, jazz bands and produced more than forty recording projects.

Dr. Wattenbarger's office was located at the entry door off the quadrangle in the prestigious Derryberry Hall, named after the college president during that time. Dr. Everett Derryberry and his wife Joan were patrons of the arts in our "Camelot" world of music. Upon entering the building, it was as though you were walking past the principal's office. Each morning one could find Doc Wattenbarger ready to start his day holding a cup of black coffee.

He would greet me with a gentle, "Good morning, Jim." During my four-year stay at the university, I never told him I preferred James as my name. If "Jim" was good enough for him, it was good enough for me!

From 1973 through 1977, approximately fifty-five music majors came from all over the country to study music education at Tennessee Tech University. Dr. Wattenbarger had assembled a faculty reminiscent of a Renaissance "court of royalty" to teach us.

Our professors were first-rate instructors, tops in their field. The instrumental, the vocal, the strings, and percussion teachers demanded the best from every student. Our curriculum was rigorous and demanding. Our ensembles in every area were top-notch. You had to practice your craft to survive at school. Music theory, music history, ensembles, ear-training, conducting, plus other academics comprised the curriculum that we had to master before leaving this court of honor. I failed to mention *piano proficiency!*

Looking back, I find it interesting that most of our teachers had German names, Wattenbarger, Hoepfinger, Bartles, Brahamstedt, Jager, Rasmussen, a Danish surname, etc. Dr. Wayne Pegram, Mr. Dan Hearn, and others, rounded out the music faculty. Talk about world-class instructors!

My first trip to Nashville was to attend a concert at the Opry House in 1974. Presented by the Nashville Symphony, the performance featured the great clarinetist, Benny Goodman. I attended the concert after being recommended by Professor Hearn, who played clarinet for the symphony at that time. I remember TTU students going backstage after the performance getting autographs from Mr. Goodman. Like Benny Goodman, Mr. Hearn was a supreme musician, a man of great stature, and a teacher who loved his students. He was challenging but gentle, demanding but kind, severe but humorous. He was a giant amongst his peers! Mr. Hearn was my clarinet instructor and mentor. My lessons were difficult as he demanded practice, perfection, and improvement each week.

As a student I played in a Woodwind Quintet and Clarinet Choir, and was part of the Tennessee Tech Symphony Orchestra for portions of my junior and senior years. I had the privilege of performing as part of a Doc Severinsen and a Roberto Flack concert. Those were big deals since only Mr. Hearn and one other student player were part of the concert orchestras. All Mr. Hearn's students respected him and never wanted to disappoint him in their skills. I presented a junior and senior recital which he pushed me to perform at my highest-level playing abilities.

In 2016, I drove back to campus to memorialize Mr. Hearn. His funeral was held at First United Methodist Church in Cookeville. The church was filled with many musicians and several classmates, whom I had not seen in years, and reminded me of the greatness of my mentor. We came to pay our respects to Mr. Hearn, our father, our mentor, our teacher, and our friend. I am so blessed to have received my music education degree from Tech. When I drove onto the campus that day of Mr. Hearn's Homegoing Service, tears of joy filled my eyes as I reminisced about the many music educators who impacted my music career.

Since then, I have taken bands back to march in homecoming parades and participate in composer's clinics, and had former students matriculate through Tennessee Tech to become music educators. I was fortunate enough to attend Dr. Pegram's retirement banquet in 2003. I asked him, "What were you thinking about to have an African American kid lead the Tennessee Tech Golden Eagle Marching Band in Fall1975 and Fall1976 in Cookeville, Tennessee?" He replied, "I chose you because you were the best."

I was invited in 2019 to attend a two-day event honoring Dr. Wattenbarger, the man who assembled such a stellar faculty and inspired so many music students. Those years he served as Chair of the Music Department are often referred to as "The Golden Years," although I prefer to call the four years I attended TTU "The Camelot Years." We shared reminiscences about those years at a recent music department reunion. The stories told by my fellow graduates, friends, and members of the Phi Mu Alpha fraternity and Mu Phi Epsilon sorority attested to the long-lasting influence of our music mentors.

Thank you, Tennessee Tech, for giving us all the gift of MUSIC!

CHAPTER 19:

Breaking Down Barriers

My journey to becoming a musician was not an easy one. The challenge of systemic racism was a constant struggle. How could I feel human or equal when laws mandated Blacks were not allowed in "Whites Only" establishments or that we had to go into back alleys to get an ice cream cone or we had to sit in the back of the bus? How could I feel like an average person when seated on the balcony of a theater and having to use filthy toilets in the public restrooms in the courthouse? I could still remember how, at an early age, our daily walk to school had been rerouted because we were being called "niggers" and "coons."

My first realization that I could break down racial boundaries came in the ninth grade. The Greeneville High School Band accepted an invitation to march in the Sugar Bowl Parade in New Orleans, Louisiana. Tennessee was playing Army! What an honor! I remember the buses loaded up with instruments, suitcases, and uniforms, and I was off to my first big adventure with my high school band.

Our band buses arrived at Meridian, Mississippi, for a rest stop and a breakfast break during the trip. Three buses filled with band kids and chaperones invaded this truck stop. Most of the Black kids sat at the same table since we were all part of our same neighborhood. There was a certain "stick-to-getherness" when we traveled. As we sat at our table and waited patiently for food orders, we noticed that the Whites in our group had been served, had eaten their meals, and were ready to load onto the buses for departure. We became disturbed and troubled as well as embarrassed. We saw our band directors and chaperones talking to the kitchen staff when someone from the establishment pointed to a sign stating, "No Coloreds Served." Our band director graciously directed us to get on the bus; and, at the next bus stop, a few band parents bought us food to eat on the bus on our way to New Orleans.

After that incident at the truck stop and during the long ride to New Orleans, all sorts of thoughts came to mind. The ride gave me plenty of time to ponder my musical career. I knew I planned to attend college and become a band director. But the total truck stop experience had changed me. I realized the many ways a band director could influence lives. I saw the compassion and kindness that my band director and other chaperones exhibited during this incident. Their charge was to take care of every kid on that trip, and they did. I wanted to emulate the caring and concern they displayed to the students, reinforcing in their actions a belief in dignity, esprit de corps, creativity, and, most important, the students' deep passion for music.

My memories took me back to the bus trip to Murfreesboro for Drum Major Camp. The "Man on the Mountain" had told me that my life would impact many. I would have a life filled with the joy of leading people to music. He continued to proclaim as he prayed for me that I would give the gift of music to the world only if I always kept God first. Would his prophetic vision come true? This band trip to New Orleans seemed like a pilgrimage giving me time to sort out my plans.

I remembered Miss Farnsworth, a local music teacher, who accompanied me on the piano at my first solo and ensemble festival at East Tennessee State when I was in seventh grade. I received a superior rating for playing a solo on my clarinet. I was so thrilled. Because of my music teachers, I received an honor in the eighth grade as I auditioned and made All-East Tennessee

Junior High and later placed in the Senior High band clinics. I was the only child of color that had achieved this honor. At the end of my eighth-grade year, I knew that I would become a music teacher! I had found my destiny.

I would later attend music clinics that reinforced my aspirations to become a music teacher. These clinics trained students to go way beyond the call of duty in working with band members and included leadership classes in their curriculum. I still remember the motto: "Don't Ask Anyone to Do Anything You Wouldn't Do Yourself,"–basically, "lead by example."

During my high school career, I received numerous awards for playing the clarinet. I started playing piano for youth choirs in Greeneville and Johnson City. I became president of the district United Methodist Youth Fellowship. Then I ran for Student Council President and was elected. I was selected to represent Greeneville High School for The Presidential Classroom for Young Americans Conference, a week-long leadership event in Washington, D.C. With my high regard for these new leadership roles combined with developing musical skills, I confirmed my destiny.

Mr. Proffitt, Mr. Treadway, Miss Farnsworth, Mrs. Goins, Mr. Winfree, and Miss Grayce Bradley were inspirational. Yet it was Mr. Treadway who allowed me to be the drum major for the Greeneville Junior High marching band in the ninth grade. Then Mr. Proffitt made it possible for me as a senior to lead the Greeneville High School's marching band. Later, Dr. Wayne Pegram would name me to lead the incredible Tennessee Tech Marching Band during the fall of my junior and senior years at Tennessee Tech in 1975 and 1976. I became the first African American to hold all these posts. It was ONLY in 1964 when the first Black student had attended Tennessee Tech University.

All these honors stemmed from my involvement with music. Music gave me a pathway to break down many of the walls of injustice that existed due to racism—and a chance to open doors for others. I became the first African American to receive honors in All Mid-State Junior High and Senior High Band competitions, to lead a prestigious marching band at Greeneville

Middle and Senior High Schools, and, most important, the first African American to lead the Tennessee Tech "Golden Eagle" Marching Band under the direction of Dr. Pegram. That was monumental.

Later in my life I continued to break barriers by way of a series of "firsts":

- First Black Band Director at White House High School

- First Black Band and Choral Director at Gallatin High School

- First Black Professor of Music and Chair of the Department of Visual and Performing Arts at Volunteer State Community College

- First Black Director of Music Ministries at Gallatin First United Methodist Church

- First Black Music Director for Tennessee to teach music education and performance in Ireland as part of the Tennessee Consortium of International Travel

- First in the Volunteer State Community College's history to be nominated for the Grammy Foundation's "Educator of the Year" (2015)

- And, most important, the first child of my parents and grandparents to receive two degrees in higher education

I believe everything I've achieved has had a purpose. Maybe my accomplishments have opened eyes and hearts and shown people of all ages and ethnicities that race does not define one's capabilities. Amazing things are possible with nurturing and perseverance; that is especially true for children. I thank God, and I thank all my family, teachers and mentors for helping make dreams come true.

THIS IS MY MIRACLE

PART III

CHAPTER 20:

Angels

Song of Inspiration: "All Night, All Day"

Read Hebrews 13:1-3

Do not forget to show hospitality to strangers, for by so doing some people have shown hospitality to angels without knowing it.

— Hebrews 13:2 (NIV)

My Grandmother Mary A. Hamilton's Story

One night, me and your grandfather, Carter, were on the way home from church. When we crossed the bridge, he saw that a storm had washed away the road ahead. Before we knew it, the flooding was upon us. Well, the car flipped over and trapped me and your mama, Naomi, underneath. She was a newborn, a little thing. I held her close to my chest, and the water poured into the car. Something must've hit me and knocked me unconscious.

Your grandfather was a strong man. He had to decide whether to save little bitty Naomi or me. Well, he says he hoisted the car off me and *pulled me to safety. But my baby wasn't in my arms. She was floating down the rushing waters. Your grandfather said that he saw some shadow of a man standing upon the bank. Dangerous as it was, the man jumped in and swam to try to save your mother. After successfully retrieving my baby, he then laid her on the bank. Your grandfather tended to me, but when he turned to thank that man, he was gone. Just like that, he was gone. I don't even know his name.*

If it weren't for that man that saved your mama, you wouldn't be here today (M. Hamilton, personal communication, 1970).

This story of faith told by Black mountain folks in East Tennessee chronicles tragedy and good fortune. Everything in between is as beautifully intricate and peculiar as the mountains themselves. These stories and my people are deeply rooted here–tall and proud, just like the enormous, boisterous Appalachian trees with branches reaching across the sky. Life is a mystery, filled with stories of uncertainty, doubt, despair, faith, and hope. Some would call the mysterious man who saved my mama an angel sent from above. To others, this story may seem like a mere coincidence. One thing is sure, because of that fateful evening and that stranger's courage, I am here today as a product of what I would call a miracle, or perhaps, to many, a blessing. I believe God's divine plan was working that day, even before I was born. We know that God performs miracles every day. Was this the work of supernatural beings that we call angels? Do they walk among us? I believe so. In scripture, we see several occasions in which angels were an integral part of God's master plan. If God chooses to use these supernatural beings in His plans for us, yes, they can walk among us doing God's will. This man was an "everyday angel."

My grandfather, a man with Samson-like strength, was given the power to overcome any barrier placed before him. He had to think quickly and make a choice–to save his wife or my mother. God had it all worked out for the good of those who love the Lord. The outcome was indeed a miracle in their life, their children's lives, and even in my life. Thanks to God that I am a living witness of my parents' and grandparents' faith.

Prayer: *Thank You for the rich heritage of faith left to us by those who went before us, those who trusted You and experienced Your miraculous deliverance. Because of their willingness to share these stories of faith, we know You have appointed angels to help and protect us as well. When we look back over our lives, we recognize that You sent angels to us at just the right moments. And we know You have appointed angel work for us to do. Help us to be alert and aware of our opportunities to serve You. Amen.*

CHAPTER 21:

Perseverance

Song of Inspiration: "My Soul Has Been Anchored"

Read James 1:2-5

Let perseverance finish its work so that you may be mature and complete, not lacking anything.

—James 1:4 (NIV)

EVERY NEW YEAR'S DAY, MY cousin Cassandra Smith-Cole and I meditate on scripture and select a word that will guide us throughout the new year. After deep meditation as we began the year 2019, the word "perseverance" kept resounding within me. At the onset of that year, I had no idea that I would face so many radical changes in my life. The year was going to be a test for me spiritually, physically, and emotionally as I adjusted to the challenges of retirement from a job that I had held for forty-two years, losing family members, caring for an ailing aunt, and losing church members I truly loved and held dear to my heart. Needless to say, the year was rough.

During times of sorrow, sickness, and tribulations, my family members always have supported one another. If someone visits our celebrations, homecomings, or church services, he or she will quickly notice individual family members' closeness and become familiar with our worship styles and how we serve and praise God. Praise and worship always have been a part of my family's DNA.

In January 2019, I made several trips to East Tennessee to visit family members, some of whom were struggling with challenging health issues. While I was visiting an aunt, who was suffering from cancer's dreaded effects, her condition worsened. Within a few days of my arrival, she died. Another aunt was convalescing at the Johnson City Medical Center and was discharged from the hospital, then admitted to an assisted-living nursing facility on the night that my other aunt had died. These events were a test of faith for our immediate family and me personally. Family members gathered to pray and plan a funeral service for one aunt while getting our other aunt assimilated into her new rehabilitation facility. Our weekend together included family activities in preparation for my aunt's Homegoing Service.

In April, I drove back to East Tennessee to attend the funeral of a cousin who had died suddenly. The loss hit harder because our family had just gathered for an aunt's funeral in January. After my cousin's funeral, my sister Mary and I ate lunch, rode around the neighborhood, and visited our aunt who was being released from the nursing facility. After picking up our aunt and my two nieces, we all headed to a local restaurant for dinner. What a celebration we had that evening. The next day I planned to drive back home to Middle Tennessee.

Before departing from Greeneville the next morning, I followed my ritual of visiting relatives to say goodbye before beginning the trek home. I drove by my sister Mary's house. I noticed her car parked in the driveway, but she did not answer the door. I proceeded to call her phone. There was no answer. I then drove to my aunt's house. She said that she hadn't heard from my sister either. I got the key to my sister's house and went back to her home. Opening the door, I called out to her. She did not respond, so I proceeded up the stairs to her bedroom. There she was, lying on the floor. She already had passed. The hardest thing I had to face that day was telling her children that their mom had died.

The grief of losing close family members was taking its toll. By trying to be outwardly strong, grief was wreaking havoc inwardly on my soul. My sister and I were best friends. Born only one year apart, we were always there for each other. We shared so many childhood memories and continued to make memories throughout our adult lives. Dealing with her death, I had to be strong and rely on my trust in God to lead me through this difficult time.

The spring brought a period of depression as I tried to adjust to the tragic loss of my loved ones. By summer's end, I was seeking medical help. A grief counselor helped guide me through this dark period of sadness. I began to reassess my priorities. At a certain point, I found I could find solace by redirecting some of the pain from my losses into creative energies. I found myself immersed in writing music, journaling, and songwriting. This instinct to create unleashed a new realization of spirituality as I honed skills that I previously had no time for in my life.

As I reflect on that time, God was preparing me for more obstacles that I would face. God had already given me the word of *perseverance*, for he knew the storms that awaited me. He was preparing me with the strength I needed to weather the turbulent storms ahead, and at the same time He was testing my faith to trust Him more.

My journey continued!

Prayer: *Thank You for the precious gift of family love. While we grieve the loss of the physical presence of those we love, we are grateful for the time we had together, knowing it was a supernatural gift that only You could have given. Thank You for the strength to press on, even in those painful moments when the loss feels so real and deep. We know You are a healer of every hurt. Amen.*

CHAPTER 22:

"Love Now"

Song of Inspiration: *"Love Now (We Can Change the World)"*

Read 1 John 3:16-20

Dear children, let us not love with words or speech but with actions and in truth.

—1 John 3:18 (NIV)

For God so loved the world, He calls one and all.
Where there is doubt, faith, let us answer His call.
To a world that's hurting, we can do our part.
To spread the Word of Jesus, so let us now start.
Love now, love now, in actions, words, and deeds.
Let the love He speaks about; supply all our needs.
To go into the world and let your love shine.
Love now, and somehow, we can change the world.

—James W. Story, 2019

THE FIRST TIME I HEARD of COVID-19 was March 2020 while I was attending a staff meeting at Gallatin First United Methodist Church. We reviewed recommendations from the bishop's office for how churches should prepare for the pandemic we were about to experience.

A few weeks prior to that staff meeting, I had experienced a terrible bout with bronchitis that required a visit to the local hospital emergency room. Despite treatment, I could not seem to recover. A few weeks after staff meeting where we outlined precautionary steps we should take against COVID-19, I started feeling worse. I began experiencing uncontrollable chills and fever. My body ached all over. I could not taste my food as I tried to eat. I finally called a friend and choir member, Brenda Reed, to take me to the emergency room at TriStar Hendersonville Medical Center. My COVID-19 experience began Thursday, March 19, 2020.

After being admitted to the hospital for observation, my prognosis became dire. I proceeded to have X-rays and a CT scan of my lungs, as well as a COVID-19 test. At that time, it took approximately five days to get COVID test results.

On day five of my hospitalization, my body temperature still would not stabilize, and my lungs became a significant concern to the medical team. My condition was severe enough that I was admitted to the hospital's intensive care unit. From that point, everything seemed to go downhill. My lungs were failing, my kidneys were failing, and I began dialysis treatments. My body was shutting down, experiencing sepsis. Eventually, a feeding tube was inserted for nourishment! I spent several weeks going in and out of consciousness as my condition worsened. The hospice nurse practitioner, Laura Youngman, explained, "With him being on the ventilator for fifteen days, he required beginning hemodialysis because his kidneys had stopped working. So, his case would have been considered a pretty serious case of COVID-19" (Rudder, 2020).

I began to realize during the times I was awake that my chances for survival were slim to none. My situation was ominous. As I lay in bed with my body shrouded with tubes, I listened to the persistent sounds of the ventilator's bellows–the "boom, boom," percussive, and swishing sounds that kept a beat like a colossal bass drumbeat.

I visualized being caught up in an infinite maze, trying to get my bearings. Remnants of my life flashed before me, and the pounding of the ventilator's beat became stronger. I thought that I was leaving this physical life to enter Heavenly Life. I was frozen. I could not move. Where am I? I was trapped in this intricate maze of confusion, and I could not get out! The beating sounds were persistent as the bellows kept the air flowing through my fragile condition! I heard music that seemed familiar — a faint melody in the distance! It was as though familiar hymns were playing over and over in my mind.

Days later, the healthcare workers found out that I was a musician. As they tried to wean me from the ventilator, Brenda Reed suggested that they play music. She told them to play "Love Now (We Can Change the World)," a song that I had penned in honor of my sister, who had died in April the year before. As the music played, I subconsciously related, "*That's my song!*" The melodies, harmonies, chords, and structure seemed to lull me into a place of repose. Now the persistent pounding of the rhythm made sense to me–it became a steady beat! As the music continued, I began to emerge from what felt like a "grave" of confusion! The healthcare workers removed the ventilator, and I began breathing independently with a minimal intake of oxygen while listening to my music.

Was the music a sign as I lay in my ICU bed? Had I gone through a complete circle of life with spiritual renewal and wholeness as I listened to "Love Now"? Oh, what a feeling of peace came over me, an indescribable peace and unspeakable joy!

"Love Now" held great meaning for me. Long before the COVID-19 scare, Rev. James C. Johnson, senior pastor at Gallatin First United Methodist Church, introduced our church's mission statement based on the scripture of 1 John 3:18: "Dear children, let us love not with words or speech, but with actions and in truth." In 2019 my colleague Pamela Andrews challenged me to write an original song for our church's summer music camp based on the "Love Now" statement.

Still grieving my sister's death, a familiar passage of scripture that we learned at Vacation Bible School as kids resonated with me: "For God so loved the world that he gave his one and only Son, that whoever believes in him shall not perish but have eternal life" (John 3:16). I sat at my piano and, using the mission statement of "Love Now" and this favorite scripture from the book of John, God spoke the song into existence. The song wrote itself. The words came to me as if I were writing a love letter to my sister, followed by a child-like melody.

The piece evolved. This heartwarming song is a reminder that the world is overflowing with opportunities to meet the needs of our neighbors. It is a rich message supported by pure melodies and inspiring modulations. Heather Sharp, one of my former students now teaching at a high school in Texas, stated, "I loved seeing the moment of recognition on my students' faces when they understood the power and urgency of the text. We can make a real difference in the world if we choose to love now, right now" (H. Sharp, personal communication, 2018). Heather's high school choir was even gracious enough to make a recording of the song (http://www.jwpepper.com/myscore/JamesStory).

There were times in the intensive care unit when I was fighting against the life-saving devices, wanting the ventilator removed. When the healthcare workers played my song, I finally calmed down, and they removed the ventilation. According to the healthcare workers who saved my life, my vital signs slowly began to improve.

How could I have known that that song written for my sister and our church's music camp would be part of my miraculous healing? Since then, I have used these scriptures as my mantra to survive the deepest darkness of depression borne from grief, loss, sickness, and despair. I have found a way to turn that into joy, gratefulness, and hope for what God has done for me.

God blessed me with the gift of music as a language of healing. God gave me the *perseverance* to overcome the many obstacles I have faced the past two years. By embracing my sister's memory, the miraculous power and beauty of music played an essential role in my healing.

Prayer: *Give us faith to trust You as we pass through experiences that are dark, extended, and unexpected. Help us trust You anyhow, even when we cannot predict when or how deliverance will come. We trust that You are working things out for us and working things in us because You have told us Your love is unfailing. Amen.*

CHAPTER 23:

"Circle of Life"

Song of Inspiration: *"I Want Jesus to Walk with Me"*

I want Jesus to walk with me.
I want Jesus to walk with me.
All along my pilgrim journey,
Lord, I want Jesus to walk with me.

In my trials, Lord, walk with me.
In my trials, Lord, walk with me.
When my heart is almost breaking,
Lord, I want Jesus to walk with me.

— https://youtu.be/vIg4Th5Y1Jc

Read John 13:6-17

Jesus replied, 'You do not realize now what I am doing, but later you will understand.'

— John 13:7 (NIV)

As MY CONDITION SLOWLY IMPROVED, the palliative care nurse informed me that I would transfer to another facility as soon as I had negative results from three consecutive COVID tests. I felt that she was abandoning me. She had been my surrogate family member this entire time! She held my hand, washed my face, and encouraged me throughout my journey. It was as though she were an angel sent by God. Initial COVID testing showed uncertain results. I knew I had a long road to recovery, but I chose to have a positive outlook.

As I regained consciousness, I faced a new reality. I began to free myself from the noise that entangled me. Nights had turned into days and days into the night. How long had I been in this haze? I then realized I couldn't lift my legs. I wondered, *"Am I paralyzed?"* Oh, the trauma! Sharp pains ravaged my right thigh. I could feel but not walk, nor could I stand independently.

More than a month after I was hospitalized, I was transported via ambulance from Hendersonville to a next step facility in Nashville. Instead of being secured on a stretcher, I sat in a transport chair with body straps. Being mobile for the first time in fifty days, I experienced an extreme case of motion sickness.

When the I arrived at Select Specialty Hospital in Nashville and the attendants removed me from the ambulance, I tried to walk. I immediately fell to the pavement. I was dead weight as an Emergency Medical Services (EMS) attendant carried me to the emergency room and placed me in a wheelchair. Somehow my dialysis port was pulled loose in the process, and I started to bleed from the incision. I lost all control of my bodily functions. It was traumatic and embarrassing.

The first days at the facility were trying. My epidemiologist and nephrologist, top medical professionals, had my best interest at heart. They worked hard to set up a program for my recuperation. A nutritionist worked most diligently to transition me from nourishment through a feeding tube to a regular liquid diet! I had to depend upon healthcare workers for everything. I was helpless. An area of my skin became infected as a result of all my days lying in bed. My skin started to break down over my body. Trying to move in the hospital bed had caused scarring on my bottom. It didn't feel delightful. I transitioned in and out of consciousness because of medication.

I stayed at Select Specialty's COVID unit for fourteen days. During that time, I always felt God's presence. My room's atmosphere was filled with love and encouragement as the healthcare teams worked together–some even praying over me. Jesus was walking with me through the valley of recovery, even though there were days of loneliness.

One morning I realized that my iPad was in my bag. I had lost all my contacts on my phone since it had crashed while at Hendersonville hospital, but now I was able to start contacting the outside world and able to talk to family. One morning while I was FaceTiming with my cousin Cassandra Smith-Cole in Washington D.C., she noticed that my oxygen tube had fallen off. A nurse was in my room, and Cassandra asked if I was off oxygen. She saw that the tubing was lying on my chest, and I was managing fine. The nurse responded, "Mr. Story, let's try turning the oxygen off and monitor its need." Cassandra told me later that day that she asked God to let me breathe without oxygen during her prayer time. Then she told me, "I noticed that the tubing was lying on your chest. You must not need oxygen." That was when the nurse concurred. Was this another coincidence? I think not. We both witnessed the Healing Power of God!

I continued dialysis. Later that week, the feeding tube was closed, and I started a liquid diet. Physical therapy was in its initial stages, but I still could not stand or walk. The medical team tested me three different times, and I was COVID-19 free! What great news! However, I still had challenges to overcome. My days became days of prayer and meditation with God, days filled with gratefulness. I began to speak with family daily via FaceTime. My most immense joy was spending devotional and prayer time with my cousin Cassandra.

On May 8, I was transferred to Sumner Regional Medical Center's Rehabilitation Unit in Gallatin. The EMS ride was a bit smoother this time. I was so excited to see the ambulance merge onto Vietnam Veterans Boulevard on the way to Gallatin. At one point during my COVID-19 journey, I thought I would never see home again. On the first night at Sumner Regional, I knew I had taken my first giant step on my road to recovery. Even though patients couldn't have visitors, I felt I was on my way home.

On the first day at Sumner Rehabilitation, the physical therapists began working on my mobility. As I tried to stand, my legs shook like a newborn lamb's. I had no strength. I looked at the palms of my hands, which appeared to have the texture of a cracked, severely weathered piece of papyrus paper. It was like looking at an ancient map of the Holy Land! I looked at my feet. They had changed to a gray color, and the soles of my feet were cracked like crumpled paper. I later asked a nurse for Vaseline. She entered the room with a basin of water, towels, and Vaseline in hand. She began to scrape my feet to remove the dried skin. Without any luck initially, she continued the process. My feet appeared as though I had been walking in the desert for more than forty days!

After the cleansing was over, the nurse poured mouthwash over my feet. Puzzled, I asked, "Why?" She responded that any brand of mouthwash could serve as an antiseptic! As she progressed, my feet became clean. This whole process was humbling. The experience reminded me of Holy Week's Maundy Thursday services when we commemorated Jesus washing the disciples' feet before the Passover meal. It felt as though the nurse was cleaning away my old skin for new skin to grow. Growth is a significant part of the circle of life. Jesus wants us to renew ourselves in His Spirit. I began to weep.

Remnants of reality were coming back to me. I kept hearing someone's phone ringtone of the opening song of the Broadway musical "The Lion King" in another room. The familiar tune pierced the air on each phone call! Sung in Zulu, the most widely spoken native language in South Africa, the famous first line of the song is an African proverb which translated into English declares, "Here comes a lion, father."

Was this another sign? The selection "Circle of Life" was a choral arrangement performed in many of my musical performances. The music played over in my mind as the vivid scenes filled my senses with beautiful landscapes of the African desert in all its splendor. The Father was with me. I felt His presence walking with me with my cleansed feet.

Prayer: *We trust that You will reveal Yourself and Your will to us as we are moved out of darkness to light and an understanding of Your perfect plan for us. Help us to grow in willingness to be conformed to Your image and to be used by You. Amen.*

CHAPTER 24:

"Sweet Hour of Prayer"

Song of Inspiration: "Sweet Hour of Prayer"

Read 2 Chronicles 7:11-18

If my people, who are called by my name, will humble themselves and pray and seek my face and turn from their wicked ways, then I will hear from heaven, and I will forgive their sin and will heal their land.

— 2 Chronicles 7:14 (NIV)

IN MY UNCONSCIOUS STATE, DREAMS would play in my head like an old movie reel, spinning and provoking memories. The vivid memories played like movies in real-time. Some scenes were reminiscent of my childhood days. I could see me and my sister playing on the playground, swimming, and attending camps on hot summertime days in the mountains. No matter what we were doing, we were summoned to our grandmother's house by 4:00 p.m. on Wednesdays to deliver her famous sugar cookies to the sick and shut-ins in the neighborhood. Then, we attended a mid-week prayer service at Tate Chapel United Methodist Church.

I remembered the aroma from the brown bags of freshly baked cookies we delivered to the minister, Reverend B.F. Johnson. I heard the special sound of our footsteps as we walked across the 1880s wood floor. I listened as the same ladies sang and prayed and testified to God's goodness.

I relived my grandmother whispering to us to get down on our knees to pray. We whispered back to her that we didn't know what to say. She replied, *"You both know the Lord's Prayer?"* We told her, *"Yes."* We never wanted to disappoint our grandmother. We both knelt and recited the Lord's Prayer in unison! After the prayer, there were thunderous handclaps and amens!

My grandmother taught us that prayer was essential in our lives. Prayers were about giving thanks to Almighty God for all the marvelous things that He had provided for all of us–our food, our clothing, our shelter, our health, and the ability to see one more day of living and breathing. She continued to tell us that prayers were a way to speak with God and reminded us that her great-grandparents had to sneak away to have church and pray because it was not allowed in their time.

As I lay in my hospital bed clinging to life, I felt the power of prayer as an aura of security surrounding me. Individual and corporate prayer were a critical part of my healing. Later I began to receive cards and notes of encouragement, but prayer preceded those tangible good wishes. Many people continued to pray for my recovery as COVID-19 affected more and more people directly and indirectly in our communities.

I learned later that businesses, restaurants, schools, and even churches closed for weeks, as directed by city and state proclamations, to slow down the spread of COVID-19. The dreaded illness was stretching hospitals to their physical limits and people were dying from the virus. Stories were circulating about people becoming sick, and — unable to be visited by loved ones — dying alone in hospitals and nursing facilities.

Even people who avoided the illness were not exempt from COVID's evil effects. More and more people were feeling isolated by the shelter-at-home directives, loss of their jobs, and loss of loved ones. Yet people were hanging on to hope, and prayer became more important than ever in our lives.

Some of my friends set up a Facebook page and began a prayer vigil for me. Members of my immediate family initiated prayer groups in East Tennessee, and my church family did the same at Gallatin First United Methodist Church. During our weekly Wednesday night rehearsal hour, my choir members lit candles to pray for me and others facing this new reality. Colleagues and others worldwide were praying for healing as the COVID-19 cases and the death rate continued to rise! One of my friends declared, "If prayer can heal you, I am now a Believer!"

My grandmother said it best in those prayer meetings of my youth as her rich dark velvety tones would rise to the rafters of that little side room at the church. I could still hear her as she bellowed out the old gospel song, "Pray for Me."

Prayer: *Thank You for the power of prayer. Thank You for those You have called and appointed to pray for us. And thank You for the miracles You have performed because of the persistent, consistent, fervent prayers that surround us. Help us to take seriously the work of prayer in our lives and in the lives of those You have placed in our lives. You are a prayer-answering God. Amen.*

CHAPTER 25:

Face to Face

Song of Inspiration: "We Shall Behold Him"

Read 2 Corinthians 4:1-18 (NIV)

Therefore, we do not lose heart. Though outwardly we are wasting away, yet inwardly we are renewed day by day. For our light and momentary troubles are achieving for us an eternal glory that far outweighs them all. So, we fix our eyes not on what is seen but on what is unseen since what is seen is temporary, but what is unseen is eternal.

— 2 Corinthians 4:16-18

MY LIFE HAS CHANGED—HOW MUCH life has evolved since March 19, 2020! My COVID journey has been a trip of unimaginable proportions and emotions. Broken into tiny little pieces of so many elements that all the "king's horses and all the king's men could not put me back together again." However, my "Humpty-Dumpty" moment has turned out differently than this nursery rhyme. It took many friends, acquaintances, healthcare workers, and family to come together in harmony to pray!

Prayers, positive thoughts, and meditation somehow came together to pick up the pieces and miraculously put my health on the right path. Without the prayers reaching the message room of God, I would not have had a chance. I was alone, down and out, could not walk, could not eat, and could not communicate for an entire month. Time seemed caught in the stillness of each moment, yet its pure peace could not be perceived. Each moment seemed like an infinity as I faced the reality of my condition. My thoughts wandered. I recognized the importance of life and realized the Master calms all human habitation to reach His heavenly domain. Was I not ready yet? Was I not good enough to enter the Heavenly realm? Such suppositions crossed my mind, but none of them consumed me with pity.

The road seemed impassable, but by drawing upon all the musical melodies stored in my mind I was able to find peace. I tried to cling to songs or anything familiar from my memory's playlist. I was struggling for normalcy in my thinking, but my brain seemed unable to process what was happening. Oh, what confusion! Pulling from every source of my being for a response, tunes continued to play like an unending musical loop in my head. I sought songs to give me the strength to endure.

With that decision to seek out songs of faith, I found solace. My inner spiritual life was becoming renewed. During this whole process of struggling, I saw a vision. I felt as if I were in a grave, and I was trying to pull myself up to the sunlight. And once I got to the top, I felt as though I was face-to-face with God, and He was reaching down His hand to me. All I could do was bow down and worship. I saw God in His full raiment. I felt that this encounter with God gave me a renewed experience of His Majesty, Grace, and Holiness. I was present in His throne room basking in His Glory.

During my time in the valley of COVID-19 darkness, I saw the face of God. He was my shepherd and my guide. All I could do was relish His awesomeness. I knew that He was speaking to me as He reminded me that I still had work to do on this earthly journey. I felt the peaceful pastures around me. I found comfort in knowing that He was going to continue to give me peace! The peace provided me with ease and joy in knowing that He is God and Lord of All. He revealed, during my time in this valley, that He would lead me along a different path to a road surrounded by new possibilities for sharing my story of His miraculous healing. I took advantage of the time to meditate in His presence.

Prayer: *Help us to fix our eyes on those things that are unseen. Keep us in that place of spiritual seeking where we look every day for what is revealed to us by Your Spirit. We confess that we are often distracted by the mundane matters of life. Help us focus on what is important to You and use us to accomplish Your purpose each day. Amen.*

CHAPTER 26:

The Valley

Song of Inspiration: "He Leadeth Me: O Blessed Thought"

Read Psalm 23

He maketh me to lie down in green pastures: he leadeth me beside the still waters.

—Psalm 23:2 (KJV)

MY GRANDMOTHER USED TO SAY, "Prayer, she is your welcome." Have you ever considered the 23rd Psalm as a prayer? It is one of the Bible's most beautifully written prayers with its poetic imagery of a shepherd protecting his flock and gently leading them through the valley of peace, thirst, discipleship, fear, and consolation. It is a prayer which resonates with many.

I realized during my illness that I was in the valley of sickness. In that valley, I had to call upon my shepherd to guide me through the many obstacles that would entangle me so that I could move on to appreciate the mountaintop experiences of life! My shepherd led me out of my bondage of despair to his peaceful valley of the light!

When I was at death's door, He brought me through. "Through" is the operative word in this passage. I remembered the night when I was on the verge of a breakthrough. I was at death's door. I began to see the faces of those who were going to be left behind. Was it the student who told me, *"Get Up, Mr. Story,"* or the former student I imagined wiping my face with a cold cloth and holding my hand, or the conversations with my two nieces and nephew? I knew I had to recover. I knew and felt the presence of prayer. And then there was the palliative nurse who whispered words of hope to me each night! *"You're going to make it."*

The 23rd Psalm prayer's key phrase is "Yea, though I walk through." For a minute, the grave consequences of dying are what scares most people. Many have asked me if I was afraid? My resounding response: *"No!!"* There is a sweet reconciliation in knowing that God is with you, and He will never leave you nor forsake you because He will walk with you through the valley of pain. He will walk with you through the valley of grief. He will walk with you through the valley! "He walks with me, and He talks with me, and He tells me I am His own. The joys we share as we tarry there, none other has ever known" (Miles, 1913).

When the peace of the still waters ran across my face, I could breathe a sigh of relief to find the answers to submitting my whole persona to God. I was not alone in my valley! What a wonderful time it was–time alone with Him basking in His glory and His Light shining through with its luminous brilliance, blotting out the darkness!

The words of Marlin D. Harris, Senior Pastor at New Life Church in Decatur, Georgia, resounded with me as I contemplated my condition and I walked through my valley. Those words created a framework for what God was teaching me.

When you have trouble in the valley, it's not yours alone. God wants to give you peace to experience the promises He has given us. When we listen, we can follow the paths that He has in store for us! When our cups begin to run over, these are blessings that He has in store for us in His Divine Plan. This symbolic meaning of the cup running over is the gateway to pass the test. That test is to trust God. Don't stay in the valley. Go through the valley! One must go through valleys before your cup can run over. Let your cup run over by exhibiting joy, hope, and kindness. When you feel the goodness of God, only then can you pass the test. Don't stay in the valley you are going through. In the valley, trust God. There is a blessed assurance that God is with you (Harris, 2012)!

When you are going through the valley, rename your valley! Rename it to receive the fullness of His blessings! When you can't find your way, your way out, God will step in on time and extend His hand and not let you fall!

- If you're in the valley of grief, rename your valley to remembrance.
- If you're in the valley of sickness, rename your valley to healing.
- If you're in the valley of sorrow, rename your valley to joy.
- If you're in a valley of despair, rename your valley to hope.
- If you're in the valley of brokenness, rename your valley to wholeness.

God will work behind the scenes when you're in the valley. He uses all of us to give others the strength to walk through their valleys! Only then will we have favor with God. Your goal should be staying on the path and following the shepherd. Where He leads us, we should follow, and when He calls our name, we will answer!

Prayer: *Thank You for the assurance of Your power to bring us through the shadowy places of life. As threatening as they may seem, we recognize that You have gone before us and cleared the way for us to pass through our troubling experiences and to experience the joy of victory on the other side. You are our shepherd, leading, guiding, protecting, directing, providing. Amen.*

CHAPTER 27:

My Battle with COVID-19 Timeline

Song of Inspiration: "The Battle Is the Lord's"

Read Psalm 34:17-20

The righteous cry out, and the Lord hears them;
He delivers them from all their troubles.

— Psalm 34:17 (NIV)

FRIENDS KEPT RECORDS OF MY progress, and I began noting how I was feeling and what was happening around me as soon as I was able. Our combined accounts of my hospitalization and rehabilitation paint a picture of my COVID-19 struggles.

Day 1-Thursday, March 19, 2020

- Arrived at TriStar Hendersonville Medical Center's Emergency Room with chills and fever
- Admitted for observation
- Tested for COVID-19 and had X-rays and CT scan

Day 5-Monday, March 23, 2020

- Waiting to see if my temperature would stabilize
- Placed in the intensive care unit at 3:00 p.m. due to issue with lungs
- Put on the ventilator at 5:15 p.m. due to breathing issues
- Established a PICC line to administer medications

Day 8-Thursday, March 26, 2020

- Received positive result for COVID-19 test
- Had a temporary catheter installed for dialysis

Day 15-Thursday, April 2, 2020

- Continued to rely on ventilator in ICU to breathe
- Suggestion was made to palliative care nurse practitioner that the staff play music to calm me as they worked to wean me off the ventilator
- Friend suggested playing "Love Now," a song I wrote in June 2019

Day 20-Tuesday, April 7, 2020

- FINALLY, the ventilator was removed and I was placed on oxygen
- Retested for COVID-19
- Due to difficulty swallowing, a GI tube was placed in the nose for feeding and medications

Day 23-Friday. April 10, 2020

- Improved enough to be moved to a regular hospital room
- Still receiving a small amount of oxygen

Day 32- Sunday, April 19, 2020

- Condition improving, but still receiving a small amount of oxygen

- Still waiting for the three negative COVID-19 tests required to move to a "next step" facility in Nashville
- Received a feeding tube due to difficulty swallowing
- Permanent catheter installed for continued dialysis

Day 36-Thursday, April 23, 2020

- BIG DAY! Moved to next step facility, Select Specialty in Nashville
- Continued dialysis and swallowing tests

Day 46-Sunday, May 3, 2020

- This is Day 10 at Select Specialty.
- I'm feeling better.
- I type my first Facebook entry in a long time.

Day 47-Monday, May 4, 2020

- I CONQUERED A MAJOR HURDLE!!! I passed the swallowing test and can have liquids!
- I was taken off portable oxygen.
- I realize my right thigh and foot have no feeling.
- I'm reminded that I STILL HAVE WORK TO DO!!!!!

Day 48-Tuesday, May 5, 2020

- Nurses keep me laughing.
- Nurses and physical therapists continue to sing to me.
- Doctors start to smile as they enter my room.
- The dialysis continues.

Day 50-Thursday, May 7, 2020

- ANOTHER HURDLE PASSED!!!!! I moved to Sumner Regional Medical Center Rehab Unit in Gallatin!!

- My goal is to become independent enough to return home with or without assistance.
- My release date will be determined by the rehab facility and doctors.

Day 51-Friday, May 8, 2020

- Stood today and took two steps
- Moved from the bed to a wheelchair with assistance
- Tried to shave—that didn't happen
- Let *perseverance* finish its work

Day 55-Tuesday, May 12, 2020

- Walked for one minute with a walker... twice
- Had permanent catheter removed
- Graduated to thicker food after another swallow test

Day 59-Saturday, May 16, 2020

- Physical and occupational therapy continue each day.
- In nine days, I've gone from not being able to stand or walk to being able to walk with a walker and now doing two repetitions of 50 feet (total of 100 feet).
- I'm working toward dressing and grooming myself.
- I reward myself with popsicles!
- I had a wardrobe malfunction the other day in therapy as I walked right out of my sweats. Yes, there is a video!
- I'm building excellent relationships with healthcare workers.
- One of my former students is my nurse who takes care of me.
- The food is delicious after coming off the feeding tube, passing my swallowing tests, and now enjoying a regular diet.
- I think I've mastered Wheelchair 101: This should be a mandatory class for Baby Boomers!

- The doctor told me that only 10% of patients with my COVID-19 experience are alive, which puts life in perspective. Please continue to pray for those who are fighting this disease.

- It's time to get our Praise on!

Day 63-Wednesday, May 20, 2020

- I have progressed to being able to walk with a walker for three repetitions of 80 feet (total of 240 feet).

- I now have 100% shower and restroom efficiency.

- I've achieved 100% ability to groom and dress in a seated position.

- I rode the stationary bike for 45 minutes yesterday (there were rest breaks every 10 minutes).

- I am able to stand for four minutes (3 repetitions).

- The Rehab Center therapists continue to kick my butt. I'll be going home very soon!!

- *People's prayers have brought healing and restoration. Music is my lifeline.*

Day 71-Thursday, May 28, 2020

- I am discharged from the local rehabilitation center.

- I am going home to complete my recovery.

Thank you, doctors, nurses, custodians, caseworkers, and technicians in all three facilities that have been part of my journey these past months. You're my superheroes and my everyday angels!

Prayer: *Thank You for enabling us to be called "the righteous" because of what Jesus did on the cross. We are so grateful that You have promised to hear us when we cry out and deliver us from all our troubles. We trust You to do what You have promised in Your word. Amen.*

CHAPTER 28:

Step by Step - Road to Recovery

Song of Inspiration: "Step by Step"

Read Matthew 17

He replied, 'Because you have so little faith. Truly I tell you, if you have faith as small as a mustard seed, you can say to this mountain, 'Move from here to there,' and it will move. Nothing will be impossible for you.'

— Matthew 17:20 (NIV)

Two months after I began my battle with COVID-19 I felt strong enough to start keeping a journal. With iPad in hand, I recorded my progress and started updating my family and friends on my status. I FaceTimed with a group of prayer partners and recorded scriptures for the day. Then a friend brought me my laptop so I could continue the book I had begun writing.

Looking back at my notes, there were some humorous as well as gratifying moments. While still at Select Specialty, the next step facility in Nashville, I mastered eating applesauce with a fork after I dropped my spoon and couldn't retrieve it.

My nurses at Select Specialty were very comical, and they kept me laughing! They woke me up singing, "You Are My Sunshine." It was 6:30 a.m. It was a generous gesture, but they couldn't find the key to the song! I sat up in the "Big Chair" for exercises...baby steps! I passed a swallow study to determine my readiness for regular food–PASSED!! Then, on to meditation, meditation, meditation!

May 8th was my first day in the SRMC Rehabilitation Unit, and I stood up! I actually took two steps. Wow! I moved from the bed to a wheelchair (with MAJOR assistance). I hadn't thought of swinging my legs in a long time! Marching band "heel-toe, left-right": I knew this one! There was an entire team of specialty doctors and therapists working for me and cheering, "You can do it!" Priceless!

I recorded a wardrobe malfunction. I lost my shorts while trying to balance myself on a walker. There are pictures! Whew! By this time, I had a Black Santa look, so I tried to shave, not too successfully the first time.

These folks understood their art of healing! The typical day included a schedule of five hours of exercise split with medical procedures. I learned how to stroll with a walker a la Tim Conway on the old *Carol Burnett Shows*.

On May 16th, I wrote my friends:

> *It has been one week and two days since arriving at this rehabilitation facility. I cannot tell you how professional these frontline warriors have been! I have enjoyed reading the multitude of notes and cards that you have sent to me. I am overwhelmed by your words of encouragement!*
>
> *...Please keep praying and positive thoughts coming, my friends. I'm so grateful!*
>
> *Thank you so much!*

Prayer: *Help us to be grateful for the little things, to rejoice in the small steps, and to know You are always working in us to bring about Your perfect plan of development. Give us the patience to trust that You will do big things with the little we have if we are willing to surrender to Your plan, Your purpose, and Your timing. Amen.*

CHAPTER 29:

Moments of Encouragement

Song of Inspiration: "God Will Take Care of You"

Read Deuteronomy 31:1-6

Be strong and courageous. Do not be afraid or terrified because of them, for the Lord your God goes with you; he will never leave you nor forsake you.

—Deuteronomy 31: 6 (NIV)

My Facebook Entry - May 17, 2020

I post these moments on Facebook to show my gratitude for each person who sends me daily messages of hope. These well-wishes have been a part of my healing process and journey.

I'm grateful. The medical staff at all three facilities on the frontline of this disease are everyday angels. They've held my hand through this entire journey. I see their faces. I hear their stories. I see the weariness at the end of their twelve-hour shifts. Some are so tired they can hardly change their plastic gowns and rubber gloves as they leave one room and go to the next. They record meds, deliver food, and change linens. Then they go home, get rest, and are back the next day. May God bless them.

I have been lucky enough to hear their songs! They are people who have sat by my bedside to care for me, contributing more than their medical expertise! It's a "Blessed Assurance" to have a doctor come and stand at the foot of your bed and stare and, after a moment of silence, look into your eyes and tell you that he is glad to meet a Survivor. We cried together.

I'm not out of the dark yet, but I can see the light! The world is changing. I am reminded to be encouraged for whatever you're going through. God is using you. There is hope!

My Facebook Entry — May 27, 2020

Forward, march! I am close to being released from rehab.

Medical facilities have not been allowing any visitors. One realizes that this disease must be faced in total isolation, away from immediate family and friends. Thank goodness for Facebook, FaceTime, and yes, handwritten notes and hundreds of Get-Well cards that connect me to the real world–to hear from and talk to people and find some sense of normalcy! My spirit would burst with emotion as I read encouraging words from everyday cheerleaders. All these acts of kindness and encouragement lifted my heart!

In all three facilities, I met real-life superheroes who became my family. They gave me the confidence and mindset to recover! They became my surrogate family, sharing their stories, culture, songs, and, yes, their healing art. Heroes do exist! It was interesting that I could not see faces, so the eyes of my healthcare heroes were the primary means of communication. There's an old saying that "the eyes are the window to your soul." The medical staff showed their compassion through their eyes. I could tell the stress they were under by looking into their eyes, for I could not see their entire face. They were still able to give me words of hope, encouragement, and kindness while caring for all their patients! Thank you, doctors, nurses, custodians, caseworkers, technicians in all three facilities for being my superheroes and everyday angels and being a part of my journey!

Prayer: *Thank You for the assurance that You are with us and that You will never leave us. Help us to reflect on the many times You have proven Yourself to us before. Allow us to experience Your presence, strength, and power through Your Spirit each moment of each day as we base our hope and faith on Your unfailing love. Amen.*

CHAPTER 30:

The Healing Power of Music

Song of Inspiration: "Ordinary People"

Read Matthew 14:13-21

They all ate and were satisfied, and the disciples picked up twelve basketfuls
of broken pieces that were leftover. The number of those who ate was about
five thousand men, besides women and children.

— Matthew 14: 20-21 (NIV)

BOMBARDED WITH MUSIC EACH DAY by the medical team at Select Specialty,
I felt like I was in the middle of producing and auditioning participants for
a major production. I could name it, *The Hospital Room: The Musical.* The
musical would feature the medical staff sharing their talents as they cared for
and encouraged COVID patients. The actors and singers would represent
various cultures and bring unique talents as they auditioned for their roles.

The stage is set! Let the show begin!

Scene I

The adjudicator, seated in his hospital chair, holds auditions and makes notes about the various performers. The contestants enter wearing their hospital uniforms and reflect the diversity of hospital employees.

The first contestant is a nurse singing, "It Is Well," a famous church hymn.

The hospital room is filled with staff leaving messages of hope for a COVID patient's departure day. As the nurse sings with the confidence of a seasoned professional, the room becomes silent. Everyone then files out of the room in silence, except for this one young nurse. She seems to be overwhelmed by the stress of working long and demanding shifts. The patient asks her, *"May I pray for you?"* She answers, *"Please do!"* She kneels beside the bed as they pray. Suddenly she begins to shake as the power of the Holy Spirit enters her body, and she begins to worship! She thanks the patient and then departs.

Scene II

"The Korean Attack Man," a physical therapist yelling the gospel song, "Precious Memories," enters the room. "Precious memories how they linger" is on a repetitive loop as he goes through his routine with his patient. The patient prompts the rest of the lyrics, but the therapist always reverts to the same two lines . . . and loudly! In a percussive voice, he demands, *"Lift the legs, 20 more times!"* He continues to sing "Precious Memories" as he exits the room.

Scene III

It is 6:30 a.m. when The Singing Nurses enter the room. Dressed in their scrubs, they are very chirpy. "It's time to rise and shine!" They sing in "perfect discord" the selection, "You Are My Sunshine," as they open the blinds. Their singing, very screeching, could wake a bear from hibernation. I could rename this scene, "The Screaming Cats." The song is deafening and certainly out of tune. Their rhythm is nonexistent until I give them a beat; still, rhythm is absent. Bless their hearts!

Scene IV

Callie Mae, the 91-year-old storyteller, enters the physical therapy room. Her monologue is titled "My Life at the Old Barn Dances." She tells the story about how when she was a child, her mom and dad would pack the kids and food in a wagon and go to the old barn dances for the weekend. Her father, a musician, would play fiddle all night sometimes, while the kids would sleep in the wagon under the stars. The highlight of her story is that years later, after she had married, she and her husband would continue dancing every weekend.

She exclaims that the song "Blueberry Hill" by Fats Domino was her husband's favorite song to dance to when they were teens. The patient plays the tune on his iPad. She starts to lift the dumbbells with the beat of the music. After lowering one of her arms, she apologizes for having her thumb in her mouth. She confesses that she is holding onto her dentures!

Scene V

The Native American Songstress comes into the room singing the Negro Spiritual, "Oh My Lord, I Want You to Help Me."

Her singing tone is a mixture of a country twang, a Broadway star belt, and an Appalachian folk style, with a heartfelt delivery. She has one of those "pull-them-in-off-the-street type of voices." Everyone outside the door on the third floor begins to listen and soon the audience is participating in the singing.

As she exits, her voice gets louder. Someone shouts, *"Enough is enough!"* Then, complete silence.

Scene VI

It is the 73rd birthday of the Danish physical therapist. The patient asks if the Danish birthday song is the same as the familiar American birthday melody? The therapist begins to sing in a very haunting modal scale pattern that is not recognizable. Its beauty is haunting. After singing, she says that she knows Negro spirituals. As she sings one, it is different than songs of the patient's youth but still enchantingly beautiful. She sings with beauty, grace, and charm.

During each special musical moment, I experienced love, and I embraced each of the various cultural offerings. The physical therapist shared her gospel music with me, so did the nurse who sang "*It Is Well.*" God gave me a beautiful tapestry of love, joy, and peace through these musical performances! Who knows? There may indeed be a musical on the horizon!

If I decide later in life to produce *My Hospital Room: The Musical,* these contestants will be my stars. If the musical does not pan out, perhaps I will start a Pandemic Gospel Choir.

During my journey, music's healing properties began to make sense to me. I could see how its relevance to the universe works in an organized and refined tonal structure that passes through the air with healing powers. Its melodic contour shapes our lives, while its harmony gives us balance. In the very moment of a discordant sound, music can give way to a simple chord that can leave us longing for joy and fulfillment. Tick-tock the clock, like a metronome, ticks away the seconds, minutes and hours chipping away at our mortality in this tiny chaotic life. We may want to get off the pendulum of confusion and stop . . . rest . . . and reflect on music's beauty and power. Coda. But music's complex rhythms keep us marching in time and we yield to our desire to keep up and to catch up in this hectic world.

Prayer: *Thank You for songs in the night, music that lifts our heart and our spirits to heavenly heights. Give us songs of worship and praise and thanksgiving. Accept our willing worship and allow our songs and our love to reach Your heart as we pour out our gratitude for Your miraculous works in our lives. Amen.*

CHAPTER 31:

The Recovery Process — Facebook Entries

Song of Inspiration: "I Want to Walk as a Child of the Light"

Read 2 Corinthians 4:1-18

For God, who said, "Let light shine out of darkness," made his light shine in our hearts to give us the light of the knowledge of God's glory displayed in the face of Christ.

— 2 Corinthians 4:6 (NIV)

THE WEEK AFTER I WAS released from my hospital fight against COVID-19 was a week of positive adjustment. I was in my own home space and becoming more self-sufficient each day. Significant responsibilities on my daily to-do list included sorting medications, going to doctor's appointments, receiving home health services, and undergoing a final procedure to remove my feeding tube. Although not being used, my doctor had suggested that the tube remain for at least six weeks before its removal.

My nieces and nephew arrived for a weekend visit. It was a joy to have them all under one roof as we celebrated life and reminisced about days past.

One evening my nephew showed me pictures that the doctors had sent him during my hospital stay. I was horrified when I saw myself lying in the ICU with innumerable tubes attached to my body. Yes, there had been talk of taking me off life support.

My nephew told the doctors to do everything in their power to save my life. My nephew showed much maturity, grace, and love in his decision-making. You see, just last April he had lost his mommy (my sister), so my illness had been especially difficult for all of us.

He tried to protect my privacy as many rumors had circulated about my illness. He stepped up to the challenge. He joined forces with my friend Brenda Reed, and they worked tirelessly to nurture me back to health, take care of my business affairs, and communicate with the medical staff via long distance since I could not have visitors!

I had decided to continue journaling about my experiences in order to give hope to those who need encouragement during dire medical events. I became more convinced of miracles as I looked at the pictures of me lying on bed #7 in ICU and realized I was now home and able to walk with assistance, talk, and play the piano! I thank God I'm alive!

Six weeks after my release from the rehabilitation unit, I wrote a Praise Report on Facebook.

May 28, 2020, was my release date from rehabilitation after my COVID-19 stay at Hendersonville Hospital, Select Specialty, and Sumner Regional Rehabilitation. Those seventy-one days while I was hospitalized still amaze me. Some days of recovery were positive and upbeat, while other days seemed dismal. Now more than six weeks after arriving home, a nurse from Home Health continues to visit weekly—a reminder that I'm still in recovery mode. The physical therapists' visits remind me that I couldn't even walk; but now, I can maneuver around my house, sometimes with a cane or no help whatsoever. I'm always in contact with my pharmacists, receptionists, and nurses to make sure medications and dosages don't react negatively! There are follow-up doctor's appointments with lung X-rays and pulmonary tests scheduled to monitor damage! There are visits to orthopedic doctors for an MRI and possibly steroid injections to assess why my thigh and foot are numb with pain. I must make calls to insurance companies to ensure all doctors and specialty vendors know the billing process and procedure for COVID-19 costs. This recovery is a full-time job!

Some days my back pain is so severe that I just lounge in my recliner with pain patches and a heating pad to address the pain. I wish I could say all days after COVID-19 are days filled with sunshine, but they're not. I continue to see the naysayers who refuse to take this pandemic seriously. It frustrates and angers me because I don't want anyone to go through this illness. The worst part is seeing people die from this disease. I'm one of the blessed ones who survived. Some people who test positive for this virus are dead within days of their diagnosis. Others are in hospital ICU units, holding on to their lives, often dying alone with only dedicated healthcare workers holding their hands as they transition.

What we are dealing with is not a political issue. It's medical and it's statewide, national, and global! Until everyone realizes this point and takes steps to eradicate this illness, we have a long road ahead. It's unpredictable! I'm not promoting any political agenda. I'm only purporting what I know and common sense!

I've had doctors who are amazed at my recovery thus far . . . yet state that no one knows the long-term ramifications of COVID-19! This doesn't scare or worry me . . . I know miracles happen every day, and I'm one of the recipients of God's tremendous power of healing. The reality of this disease: It is deadly. The infection numbers are on the upswing daily, and it's our human responsibility to be diligent in practicing the protocols recommended to us in order to live and stay well. Wearing a mask is a distraction and can be uncomfortable, but it is one step toward saving humanity and not allowing the coronavirus to spread! I have spoken with and encouraged so many survivors and prayed for their healing! Let's *continue to lift up those folks and their families with positive thoughts and prayers as we all weather this storm together.*

My seventh-week Praise Report revealed further healing.

Today marks seven weeks after spending seventy-one days in the hospital recovering from COVID. I am on the road to recovery! The statement, "healing is a marathon, not a sprint," made by the celebrity Dr. Phil on some TV show I watched, is indeed true. I was not confident I could post the first picture of my hospitalized self; but, in my heart, I had to do it for the sake of those who believe that COVID is a hoax and those who refuse to practice the safety protocols for staying healthy! Imagine spending an entire month in ICU and fifteen days wearing this contraption! It's not a political ploy to wear a mask to help curtail this disease if you're saving someone's life! As I hear about and see others die—knowing it could have been me, I'm personally insulted that some people have such deep disregard for "love thy neighbor" and won't take simple steps to help their neighbors survive! Today is the day to step up and live!

I recorded a great day at the doctor's office.

When the cardiologist says to you in an appointment, "COVID-19 may have done a lot to your body, but it didn't touch your heart," it's a great day! There were two grown men crying tears of joy in his office!

Prayer: *Thank You that even as we confront the challenges we do see, You are working behind the scenes to build a hedge of protection around those things that are essential to our health and well-being. Thank You for protecting us from dangers seen and unseen. Open our eyes and hearts to understand the depth of Your love for us. Amen.*

CHAPTER 32:

Short Journal Entries

Song of Inspiration: "Open the Eyes of My Heart"

Read Ephesians 1: 17-21

I pray that the eyes of your heart may be enlightened in order that you may know the hope to which he has called you, the riches of his glorious inheritance in his holy people, and his incomparably great power for us who believe. That the power is the same as the mighty strength.

—Ephesians 1:18-19 (NIV)

Mr. Independence's Driving Adventures

I've been addressing eye problems with an ophthalmologist. I have not attempted to drive for the last four or five weeks because I'm seeing double. Yesterday, however, I decided to drive myself to a doctor's appointment in Hendersonville. After a two-hour meeting, I was excited that I made it to the appointment on time. I was so excited, driving myself! Wow!

I decided to pick up dinner at a local restaurant. While waiting in the take-out area, I decided to play some jams on the radio. The sun was shining and I had the windows rolled down; I had on my cool shades taking in some natural vitamin D! The food arrived, and as I was driving off, my car stalled. Sitting in the middle of the road, I heard an elderly gentleman yell to me to put my car in neutral, and he would push me out of traffic. The gentleman pushed as hard as he could, almost to the point of exhaustion. Two waiters from the restaurant quickly came to assist. My battery was DOA. My car has been sitting in my garage for months; I had gasoline but no juice in my battery life! I called a friend to assist me and, after calling one of his associates whose office was nearby, he came to my rescue. My car started, and I made it home!

Today I was bold enough to drive myself to the Toyota dealership to check out the battery, and of course, I needed a replacement. I was pleased to encounter a former student who worked at the dealership. I also was humbled, as I entered the service area, by people who greeted me with kindness and were glad for my COVID recovery. I felt great, so I went to the bank.

My visit to the bank changed my mood. I had problems with the automated drive-thru machine because I made too many attempts to get money with my debit card. For some strange reason, I kept hitting "Spanish" instead of "English." Suddenly the machine messaged, "See the cashier." Ok, I looked in my rearview mirror and noticed there was no one behind me so I started to back my car out of the drive-thru service lane. As I backed out, I drove up on the curb and almost hit the bank's drive-thru barriers. I then saw the inside teller holding her face in horror. Once she saw who I was, she asked, "Are you now driving?" I responded, "It's been a while." She asked, "Do you need an Uber?" In shame, I drove home slowly and cautiously like I had seen many of my older friends and family members do. I didn't want to shame myself two days in a row!

I am ready for a nap because the Ever-Ready bunny is kaput!

The moral of these stories? Thank you, community and friends! It still takes a village to raise us old folks! Sometimes you need a good laugh!

Prayer: *Thank You for Your patience with us, even as we try to rush along in Your plan for our development and healing. Thank You for protecting us even from ourselves. We trust You, God, to do what is best for us when it is best for us. Amen.*

CHAPTER 33:

For Good

Song of Inspiration: "We Worship You"

Read Romans 8:18-30

And we know that in all things God works for the good of those who love him,
who have been called according to his purpose.

— Romans 8:28 (NIV)

NINE MONTHS AFTER MY COVID diagnosis, I began to prepare for the 2020 Christmas holidays at my church. The holiday celebrations were different due to the pandemic. I was different too, as I shared in an e-newsletter to the congregation of Gallatin First United Methodist Church.

Good? COVID Good? How could you even suggest such a thing?

Scripture tells us that Jesus prepared for phases of His life by separating himself from others to commune with His Father. Forty days in the wilderness. FORTY days! It took that long for our Lord and Savior to prepare himself for the ministry that God set before him. Those forty days were not only for Jesus' good but for the good of all humanity.

In 2020, I could not have imagined fasting and praying for forty days. Yet, in a way, I had my "wilderness experience." However, it was not by choice. As I reflect on my time in the wilderness, I believe that God was working it for my good. I felt the power of prayer. While I was unaware that it was happening, others were pleading with my Creator for my life. I had visions. Others have told me that they, too, had dreams. Several "just knew" that God was in control. "Be Still and Know That I Am God" (Psalm 46:10). Well, being still does not come easily to me. Compelled to be quiet, I felt the Holy Spirit working in me, for me, and around me. You need to know that God is alive and well in the hearts of those working in our local community. People were not afraid to pray with and over me. That is the Good News Gospel!

Nine months after my COVID nightmare began, here we are in the season of Advent. The season challenges us to prepare our hearts for a newborn savior and challenges us to wait. When I emerged from rehab, I knew that I still had a long path to full recovery. I now realize that I must continue to wait for the day when I will resume a "normal" life.

Last week I was overwhelmed as I entered our sanctuary for the first time since March for a Christmas rehearsal. Gathered with only those participating in what is to be my Christmas gift to God, the church's sanctuary, and this congregation, I realize I am not back. My hands ache, and my shoulders remind me that I am still on the path out of my wilderness. But the tears in my eyes are not from pain. They are tears of gratitude.

A day in bed following that session reminded me that my stamina has not returned. But I know that God IS working all of this for GOOD. I am learning patience. I am learning a new depth of gratitude. I am learning new ways of doing things, understanding that "good" has a new definition. Perhaps my Sculptor is re-making my image more like that of my Savior. How "good" is that?! What a Christmas gift!

I submit Sunday's musical offering in humble gratitude and hope my friends and church members receive it as a love offering. I wait with great anticipation until the day that I can fully participate with them again.

'What can I give Him poor as I am? If I were a shepherd, I would bring a lamb. If I were a Wise Man, I would do my part. Yet what can I give Him: give my heart' (Rossetti,1872).

Prayer: *Show us the good, God. Reveal the good that You are bringing out of our challenging times. When the clouds of trouble appear on the horizon, there is a breakthrough with the light of Your love. Help us to trust You even when we cannot see through our trials. Help us to trust You long enough to testify to what You were bringing to pass. Amen.*

CHAPTER 34:

Prayer, Healing, and Hope

Song of Inspiration: "The Solid Rock"

Read Jeremiah 29

'For I know the plans I have for you,' declares the Lord, 'plans to prosper you and not to harm you, plans to give you hope and a future.'

— Jeremiah 29:11 (NIV)

THE MOST SIGNIFICANT PART OF my healing has been seeing the impact of communal and individual prayer made real. Many were praying for me and praying for our country and praying for the survival of a pandemic society. They prayed for those who were ill and those who were impacted in other ways. The isolation of COVID-19 patients and isolation of their families invited loneliness and depression. Families and friends could not visit their loved ones in hospitals and nursing facilities.

Although I could have no visitors, there had been prayer vigils started by my immediate family in East Tennessee, my church family at Gallatin First United Methodist Church, and church affiliations worldwide. I learned that my chancel choir members were lighting candles on Wednesday nights to pray for me.

People have said to me that I'm lucky to be alive! That's false information! *I'm blessed to be alive!*

The world encountered a global pandemic in 2020 that continues. A pandemic is defined as "an epidemic occurring worldwide, or over an extensive area, crossing international boundaries and usually affecting a large number of people" (World Health Organization, 2011, p.1). This classical definition includes nothing about population immunity or disease severity. Seasonal epidemics can cross international boundaries and affect many people; however, seasonal epidemics in themselves are not considered pandemics.

The COVID-19 virus has spread around the globe, without regard for different ethnicities, climates, or time zones. People around the world are battling this pandemic. It's not all about us! We too often think individually instead of globally. As this book goes to press, more than 4.7 million deaths from COVID have been recorded worldwide, more than 700,000 of those in the United States, and the number keeps growing.

When asked what advice I would give people about protecting themselves from COVID, I automatically advise people to read reputable articles and substantiated research regarding COVID-19! What advice would I give to people who receive a COVID diagnosis? Lately, I have communicated with several individuals and their families about my experience with COVID. I pray with them, and for them; we text and speak on the phone. I've told my former nurses and doctors to have interested people inform me of their needs! I'm not a doctor nor do I profess to be, but I can share a word of hope and encouragement and give those who are ill the comfort of knowing that they are not alone. I contracted the virus in early March 2020! There were no defined treatments for COVID-19 approved by the CDC at that time, but significant steps have been made toward controlling and eradicating this dreaded disease. Treatment advances continue to be made.

Prayer: *We are grateful that You have a plan for us, a plan to prosper us and to give us hope and a future. We confess that we do not always understand Your plan, but we thank You that You will order the events of our lives to enable us to help someone else along the journey. Amen.*

CHAPTER 35:

A COVID-19 Survivor's Prayer

Three different hospitals in 71 days,

Would this pain ever go away?

It indeed teaches me how to pray.

Thank you, Lord, for one more day.

And on a ventilator for 15 days

In the ICU for one month during my stay.

If I had a worse enemy in this world, I hope I do not,

I don't wish this nightmare of COVID 19 that disease that I got.

Hear our prayer our God,

For you are my rock in the midst of the storm.

And give us hope for those who mourn

For friends and family

That have gone on before

I was on dialysis; now I am off.

I was on a feeding tube; now I can eat.

I had bruises on my arms and my feet.

And now

My sight is waning, but now I can truly see.

My smell is gone, but the sun still shines on me.

Afterward, my upper thigh is numb,

We thank you, Lord, for the rising of the sun.

I had to learn to walk and swallow again

But this chapter is not the end!

Forgive me, Lord, for over and over I ask

Protect Your children by wearing a mask!

Lord, hear my prayer.

Tell us what to do!

Help us, God!

To make it through.

I am weak,

But You are strong.

Give me strength to carry on.

Draw me closer, Lord to Thee!

Open our eyes that we may see,

Your healing hand has protected me!

Now I'm free! Amen.

—James W. Story, April 2021

CHAPTER 36:

From Hoax to Hope

Song of Inspiration: "Lord of the Dance"

Read Psalm 30:1-12

For his anger endureth but a moment, in his favor is life: weeping may
endure for a night, but joy cometh in the morning!

— Psalm 30:5 (KJV)

I RECALL WATCHING A MEMORIAL service in which President-Elect Biden
paid respect to the victims of COVID-19. Something resonated within me
as I listened to his message! I paraphrase, *COVID-19 does not discriminate,*
nor does the disease recognize color. It has impacted us all. COVID is not a
political statement!

I lost two incredible friends from this disease the week of this broad-
cast–a classmate from high school and a dear friend's mother, who inspired
my musicianship from middle school through my college years and still
impacted me in her adult years as she served as a church organist. I continue
to learn of friends and relatives who are ill, clinging to their lives, struggling
to live.

Some folks will try to convince others to believe: "It's only the flu!" How dare you? It's not a hoax. It's real. I won't even go into vaccination questions.

While I was hospitalized, the majority of COVID-19 patients were dying alone, without their families at their bedside. Only healthcare workers were holding their hands, giving them the last words of their passage. Bodies were racking up in morgues across the country. Air restrictions and bans were being lifted in larger cities so that morgues could cremate the dead. Sound morbid? Of course! I was almost one of these statistics! This label as a "hoax" is such a misnomer! It's factual. There is hardly anyone that has not been affected by this pandemic.

I can no longer be silent.

I can recall experiencing so many emotions as I fought for my life. I felt the deepest and darkest despair of my existence. It was one of my most traumatic experiences. It was unimaginable! For a while I wasn't sure if I was dead or alive, and I eventually realized that my options for living were running out. I heard the "boom, boom" of the ventilator as it sustained the visual remnants of my life. I thought that I was leaving this physical life to enter eternal life. I felt as though I was trapped in a maze and could not get out!

While the beating sounds of the ventilator's bellows kept air flowing through my fragile state, familiar music seemed to bring a distant and faint melody to my mind. That melody evolved into a harmony that gave me peace, and that peace gave me hope! Music and prayers gave me hope!

Remember, hope is needed in our world today. There is hope that we can eradicate this disease. Stay vigilant! As Psalm 30:5 (KJV) states, "For his anger endureth but a moment, in his favor is life: weeping may endure for a night, but joy cometh in the morning!"

Prayer: *Thank You for the promise of joy on the other side of my weeping. I understand that weeping is a part of life and that Jesus told us we would have tribulations in this life. But I am grateful that You always bring joy after suffering, peace after confusion, light after darkness. Amen.*

CHAPTER 37:

The Light and the Leaf

Song of Inspiration: "The Majesty and Glory of Your Name"

Read Psalm 8:1-9

O Lord, our Lord, how excellent is thy name in all the earth! who hast set thy
glory above the heavens.

—Psalm 8:1 (KJV)

Spring 2021 Journal Entry

A year ago, we were all looking forward to the advent of spring—
planning spring breaks, awaiting graduations, and looking forward
to Easter. Then suddenly, everything stopped. We were facing a global
shutdown due to the onset of COVID-19.

Through this journey, I have found healing and strength through
everyone's prayers, reading scriptures, and creative writing. Each morning I open my blinds to savor the dawning of a brand-new day. Outside
my living room window, there is a young maple tree. As I write this
memoir, I notice there is one single leaf on that tree. I draw parallels with

"The Last Leaf," a short story by O. Henry. But I tell a different story. This maple leaf, like me, has survived the sweltering heat of summer, the crisp coolness of fall, and a brutal, bitter winter. Now it anticipates the tree's spring budding. Today I am reminded of Ecclesiastes 3:1: "There is a time for everything and a season for every activity under the heavens."

Like the tree, we encounter the seasons, the crispness of spring rain, the heat of a summer day, the coolness of a foggy autumn morning, and the bitterness of winter's ice and snow. The one thing that is static throughout the seasonal changes is that darkness always gives way to light. We all experience dark moments in our lives, and this past year may have been darker than most. But the good news is that after night comes the light. Oh, how we love the light of morning. As we witness the miraculous changes from season to season, we know that God's Light shines eternally. This single leaf would not have survived the seasons without the strength to endure massive seasonal changes. One year equals 525,600 minutes, a lengthy amount of time for a leaf to hold onto its branches.

As I look over this past year of trials, tribulations, and victories of my recovery, I am so grateful for the blessings that I have received. Just like the leaf, I have endured.

Next week, I will release a new song, "There's a Miracle in You," written in celebration of lives touched by the coronavirus. Music expresses my faith and hope for those who have recovered and still are recovering from COVID-19. Without trust, hope, and prayer, I would not be here today. I am a living witness of God's miraculous power of healing, and so are you, the reader. We all are beginning to come out of the darkness into a season of light. The song is dedicated to all healthcare workers and COVID-19 survivors and will be available on streaming services.

Prayer: Thank You that in every season You are preparing us and blessings for us for the next season. I am so grateful for the blessings You saved for me just for this season in my life, that You have a plan for me to be maximally useful to Your kingdom. Amen.

CHAPTER 38:

"There's a Miracle in You"

When you're down and out and lonely, mired in life's empty tomb and
Feeling like there's no way out.
Darkness has no place when music fills the space
And suddenly you begin the shout
There's a miracle, waiting for you
Even in the darkness, the Lord will see you through
He'll stretch out His hands as part of His healing plan
There is a miracle in you.
When Your room is still and empty, and the silence floods your mind
You realize the need for His Grace
You turn around and see the one who sets us free
You envision that God is in this place
There's a miracle happening to you
Even in the darkness, the Lord will see you through.
He'll stretch out His hand as part of the healing plan
There is a miracle in you!
Seek ye first the kingdom of God,

All will be given unto you
Knock, and the door will be open
He will see you through
There's a miracle in you.
There's a miracle happening to You
Even in the darkness, the Lord will see you through.
He'll stretch out His hand as part of the healing plan
There is a miracle in you.

—Lyrics and Music by James W. Story, 2020

Prayer: *I surrender to Your miracle-working power. Thank You that You are not finished with me, and I confess that I have fallen short of Your glory. But I want You to reveal the miracle in me, not for my glory but Your glory. Use me today. Amen.*

CHAPTER 39:

Going Home

Song of Inspiration: "O Happy Day"

Read Philippians 4:1-7

Do not be anxious about anything, but in every situation, by prayer and peti-tion, with thanksgiving, present your requests to God. And the peace of God, which transcends all understanding, will guard your hearts and your minds in Christ Jesus.

—Philippians 4:6-7 (NIV)

ON MAY 28, 2020, I left the local rehabilitation center where I had made so much progress after leaving the hospital and next step facility! Sumner Regional's Rehab Unit was out-of-network for my insurance plan and was going to be more costly, so my insurance company had questioned why I wanted to transfer to Sumner Regional. But they approved my request.

Coming to Gallatin was a brilliant choice! It brought me home to my church and so many friends and colleagues. Hospitals were not allowing any visitors until a few days before I was released to go home. Those of us who contracted this disease faced total isolation from immediate family and friends, but I could look out a window and see familiar surroundings. Thank goodness for Facebook, FaceTime, and, yes, handwritten notes and hundreds of get-well cards that connected me to the real world. Being able to hear from and talk to people created some sense of normalcy.

I will be forever grateful to the healthcare workers whose faces were covered but who showed compassion through their eyes! They gave me words of encouragement and kindness, while building my strength! Above all, each one of them gave me hope. Since I had contracted COVID-19 so soon after the pandemic's onset, I was one of the first COVID patients they had encountered.

Thank you, doctors, nurses, custodians, caseworkers, and technicians in all three facilities for being my superheroes and everyday angels and for being a part of my journey to recovery!

To my family, church family, chancel choir, colleagues, former students, and friends, thank you for starting a candlelight vigil that ignited a miracle around the world. One single act of praise: Prayer! I'm humbled. Thank you for being there holding my hand through this spiritual journey, but most of all, thank God for His Amazing Healing Grace!

I have tried to write thank you notes so many times since I have been home. Still, every time I attempt to do so, I am so overcome with thankfulness and gratitude that my feeble hands cannot capture the right words and my eyes overflow with emotions. Tears of joy stream down my cheeks like *Rivers of Joy*!

My words may be insufficient, but my heart is full of gratitude! In his sermons, we hear from Pastor James how the power of prayer is our most accessible tool for spiritual growth on our Christian journey. I can certainly say I'm a living witness of God's Miracles.

I thought I could never survive last year, but when this storm hit, the people's prayers spoke and brought me healing despite this storm. I have witnessed the gift of PRAYERS from so many of you and people from all over the world! I know He has worked a miracle in my life!

I'm humbled in His presence!

The day I was released to go home from Sumner Regional Medical Center's Rehabilitation Unit, I felt the warmth of being home before I ever left the hospital—familiar faces, familiar voices. A group from my church choir and the New World Singers gathered and sang the gospel song, "*O Happy Day*," as I passed through the exit door. ***This was the happiest day of my life!***

Prayer: *Thank God for miracles in all our lives and thank His people worldwide who linked together in prayer during my recovery. I also want to thank Him for being able to see another day. I'm grateful for all the well-wishes for my healing! Miraculous things can happen when people humble themselves and pray. Let Your light shine through me to let others know about Your miraculous power to heal and deliver. Let my testimony help others to be encouraged to press on in faith. I want to be a walking, lit up, talking billboard for Your healing power. Amen.*

References

Atkins, J. (1735). *Voyage to Guinea, Brasil, and the West Indies in His Majesty's Ships, the Swallow and Weymouth*. London: Ward and Chandler. Retrieved from https://gallica.bnf.fr/

Brooks, T. (1984). *America's Black Musical Heritage*. New Jersey: Prentice-Hall.

Equiano, O. (1789). *The New Interesting Narrative of the Life of Olaudah Equiano*. 1-2. London, England. Retrieved from https://docsouth. unc.edu

Greene County Office of Deeds. (1910, January). Pruitt Hill Methodist Episcopal Church, certified and registered in *Greene County Deed Book* No.85, page 472, and noted in Book No. 5, page 196.

Harris, M. D. (2012, January 21). *Senior Pastor-New Life Church: Spoken Word*. Decatur, GA.

Johnson, A. J. (2018, February 8). Lone Woman Who Sat with MLK, Jr. During Columbus Bomb Threats Dies at 102. *Columbus Ledger-Inquirer Newspaper*, Columbus, GA: Article 198994154.

Miles, A. C. (1913). *In the Garden*. New York, NY: Hall-Mack Publishers.

National Parks Service. (2020). *The Slaves of Andrew Johnson*. [Brochure]. Retrieved from

https://www.nps.gov/anjo/learn/historyculture/slaves.htm

Rossetti, C. (1872). In the Bleak Midwinter. *The United Methodist Hymnal, No. 221*. Retrieved from https://www.umcdiscipleship.org/resources/history-of-hymns-in-the-bleak-midwinter

Rudder, R. (Producer). (2020). Prayer and Worship Sustain COVID Patient. *700 Club*

[Television Series]. Virginia Beach, VA: Christian Broadcasting Network, Freeform, TBN Films. Retrieved from https://www1.cbn.com/prayer-and-worship-sustain-covid-19-patient

Staples, G., Kirby, E., & Wimbish, M. Historians, GMBC, Inc. (2012). *Through the Looking Glass: Kindle Edition*. Florida: Xulon Press Christian Publishing.

Story, J.W. (1987). *Tennessee Roots: A Musical Celebration*. Nashville, TN: JSto Productions.

Story, J. W. (2019). *Love Now, We Can Change the World* [CD]. Nashville, TN: JSto

Publishing. Retrievable from https://youtu.be/sAWvo6RBIFI, https://open.spotify.com/album/4PbnhRmf3sWqhZqaxyYVeq, and http://itunes.apple.com/album/id1559351093?ls=1&app=itunes

Story, J. W. (Executive Producer). (2019). *New World Spirituals 1619-2019*-Various Artists performing African American Spirituals [CD]. Nashville, TN: JSto Productions. Retrievable from http://itunes.apple.com/album/id1492064056?ls=1&app=itunes and https://open.spotify.com/album/7z4uoeVja1iC269BG0aXHr

Story, J. W. (2020) *There's a Miracle in You*. [CD] Nashville, TN: JSto Productions.

Retrievable from http://itunes.apple.com/album/id1559351093?ls=1&app=itunes and https://open.spotify.com/album/6aCwsDJfpOZ7ElHm5y5v9B

Westmoreland, W. (Director). (2018). *Colette* [Motion Picture]. United States: Number 9 Films, Killer Films & Bold Films.

Wimbish, Minnie–100 Year Old Recites Favorite Poems (2015). Article 198994154. *Columbus Ledger- Inquirer Newspaper*, Columbus, GA. Retrieved from https://youtu.be/bP3pXHTfJOE

Woodson, C. G. (1926). Negro History Week. *Journal of Negro History*, XL. No. 2. 239.

Retrieved from https://blackquotidian.supdigital.org/bq/february-24-1934

World Health Organization. (2011, July 1). *The classical definition of a pandemic is not elusive.*

Retrieved from https://www.ncbi/nlm.nih.gov/pmc/articles/PMC3127276/

DISCOGRAPHY

LOVE NOW

(We Can Change the World)

Executive Producer
James W. Story

JSto Publishing (ASCAP)
© 2019

There Is
a Miracle
in You

NEW WORLD
SPIRITUALS
1619 ~ 2019

Executive Producer James W. Story

JAMES W. STORY

Receiving his Bachelor of Science in Music Education from Tennessee Technological University in Cookeville, Tennessee, and a Master of Music Education degree at Austin Peay State University in Clarksville, Tennessee, Professor of Music James W. Story has taught pre-school through higher education.

Story was honored by the Tennessee State Assembly, Gallatin News, and the Gallatin NAACP as the "2020 Gallatin Citizen of the Year" for his service as an educator and for his contributions through social media to connect the general public to his struggles with COVID-19 and the sacrifices of healthcare professionals who cared for him and others.

He holds membership in the National Academy of Recording Arts & Sciences Grammy Foundation and Phi Mu Alpha Music Fraternity and is currently listed as a writer for the American Society of Composers, Authors, and Publishers.

His most meaningful accomplishment was receiving a grant from The National Endowment for the Arts and Alternate Roots, Inc. to produce an original stage production, "Tennessee Roots," a musical presentation of Negro spirituals and Appalachian folk songs.

At the local community level, he has served as music director for several Broadway musicals and has conducted works for choir and full orchestra.